# Advanced Praise for
## *Everything You Need is Within You*

"As the saying goes, 'the acorn doesn't fall far from the tree.' I worked with Surinder at both Pepsi and Pizza Hut and the self-belief that his father instilled in him helped make him a world-class leader. The compelling story of his father's life and wisdom is inspirational. You never know what you're capable of. — David Novak, Executive Chairman, YUM Brands

"Surinder is one of the most thoughtful business leaders of the present. This book tells a timeless story while imparting wisdom to all ages and circumstances in a hugely relevant manner. There is not a more poignant message for us all at this time than the title of this book. Yes, we can make a difference and that should be our purpose however we choose to define it." — William "Beau" Wrigley Jr., Chairman of the Board of Directors at Surterra Wellness, Former Executive Chairman, Wm.Wrigley Jr. Company

"This book shows that life is what we decide to make it. Children from a poor village with no running water, dirt roads and no electricity rose to unexpected heights because a teacher really believed that they had everything they needed to be successful even when they hardly had food to survive. A guide for parents and an inspiration for the young who choose to make a meaningful difference in the world today!" — Bill Perez, Managing Partner, Fam-Gen, Former President and CEO, SC Johnson & Company, Former CEO, Wm. Wrigley Jr. Company

"This rags to riches story is much more about a journey than a destination. It's a story about having a strong moral compass, about perseverance, mutual support and respect. It's about the birth of the largest democracy in the world and its more recent emergence as a leading intellectual powerhouse. Kanshi Ram Arora would be very proud of his legacy." —Dr. James Prendergast, Ret. Exec Director, Institute of Electrical and Electronics Engineers

"When I was Surinder's boss at Pepsi 25 years ago, I learned more from him, than he got from me. After reading his book yesterday, the dynamic hasn't changed 25 years later." — Mike Lorelli, former PepsiCo President

"Looking for a heartfelt, authentic leadership book that conveys the message using real life stories? Then this is the book for you. Surinder's 16 principles have made a difference in my leadership, and I bet they will make a difference in yours too." — Cheri Warren, Former Board Member, National Grid USA, Former Board Chair and Head of Office of the CEO, GlobalSpec

"Surinder Kumar is an incredibly successful leader of industry, recruited to C-suite positions at five major corporations. He reveals his philosophy for achievement based on work ethic and honest effort. Tracing his roots to an impoverished, near-death childhood in war-torn India, the strong teachings of his father, Bauji, forged a family who achieved the elusive American dream. His personal first-hand account of life events is compelling, but this important writing serves as an inspirational text to guide students or immigrants who seek to make our world a better place. This professor will place this work in the library of students who should be inspired by Kumar's insights." — Dr. Ken Lee, Professor, The Ohio State University

"*Everything You Need is Within You* is a book that reminds us that simple leadership principles are forever green. Applying the 16 principles presented in this book has helped me to be a better person and leader. I have become more intentional about pursuing my life's purpose to help others realize their dreams." — Matt Loeb, Executive Leadership Coach and Former CEO

"My father Kanshi Ram Arora truly believed that everything we need to build a great life resides within us. He believed strongly in education and life-long learning. His simple principles and insights transformed a poor small village and its residents from being victims of India's Partition to victors. The book captures the key insights and shows how an inspirational leader can influence the destiny of many generations." — Om Parkash Arora, eldest son of Kanshi Ram Arora

"*Everything You Need is Within You* is such a fascinating and inspirational story of Surinder's family's personal struggle to survive. Surinder lives the principles he was taught every day. He is a testament to his father's teachings. For many, reading this book will make you grateful for where we were born. It will bring back memories of what we all have been taught as children by our parents and grandparents. It is a must read for all." — Jim Wisniewski, President, Culinary Focus/Spice Guild

# EVERYTHING YOU NEED IS WITHIN YOU

## Surinder Kumar, PhD

The intent of the author is only to offer information of a general nature to help you in your efforts toward self-improvement. In the event you use any of the information in this book for yourself, the author and the publisher assume no responsibility for your actions.

The Story Plant
Studio Digital CT, LLC
P.O. Box 4331
Stamford, CT 06907

Story Plant hardcover ISBN-13: 978-1-61188-298-8
Fiction Studio Books e-book ISBN-13: 978-1-945839-49-8

Visit our website at www.TheStoryPlant.com

First Story Plant Printing: April 2021

Printed in the United States of America

0 9 8 7 6 5 4 3 2 1

Dedicated to my father, Kanshi Ram (Arora), who spent all his life transforming his family, his village, and the lives of hundreds of other people who met him.

This book is also dedicated to the millions of Indians, including Hindus, Muslims, and Sikhs, who either lost their lives or were displaced from their homes during the Partition of India. The survivors have horror stories to tell. However, they have worked tirelessly to rebuild their lives and transform themselves from victims to victors.

> "There is no use complaining about what you do not have. Use what you have, and you will find that everything you need to be successful and happy in your life is within you. Everything that is holding you back is also within you."
> – Kanshi Ram Arora

# Contents

# Introduction

"*Master ji* (respected teacher), you need to leave the village tonight with your family," said the young Muslim student. His head bowed and his hands folded in a sign of respect, his voice trembled as he uttered these words to his teacher, my father, Kanshi Ram. "There are rumors that all Hindus living in the village will be killed and their homes occupied by the Muslims. Please leave as soon as possible and don't tell anybody that I warned you; they will kill me if they find out."

My dad drew his student close and embraced him. "Thank you very much for letting me know and for saving my family," he said. "We will make the arrangements to leave as soon as possible. Would you like some tea before you go?"

"*Nahin Sahib* (no sir). I must ask for your leave now. *Khuda Hafiz* (God be with you). I am so sorry that you have to go, but you must leave the village tonight." With these last words, the young man disappeared in the dark.

The year was 1947. Ever since the end of World War II, rumors had been circulating that India might no longer be a part of the British Empire. Britain's economy was in bad shape after the war, so they needed to divest. On top of that, the Indian population had become tired of their treatment by the British, leading to discussions of Britain's departure from India among representatives of the various Indian communities.

The Indian Independence Act, declared independence for India from British Rule on August 15, 1947. According to the Act, India was to be partitioned into two countries: India, which would be a secular nation with multiple religions, and Pakistan, which would be a homeland for Muslims. The creation of two nations would lead to millions of Hindus moving from the land allotted to Pakistan over to the new India, while several million Muslims would need to leave their homes in India to move to Pakistan. Never had such a partition and mass movement of families taken place in human history. The chaos, the unrest, and the anger associated with this boiled over, leading to an expression of animalistic violence between Hindus and Muslims who had lived as neighbors and friends just a few weeks before the Partition. While the resulting death toll remains disputed, estimates range from two hundred thousand to two million.[1] The general consensus now is that over a million people were killed in these communal clashes.

[1] Ian Talbot and Gurharpal Singh. *The Partition of India*. Cambridge University Press, 2014.

The British had ruled India in various forms. First during the 18th century under the British East India Company and then beginning in 1858 under the direct rule of the British government as British India. During that time, they'd used the resources of India for their own economic interests. They'd conscripted more than two-and-a-half million Indians into the British Indian Army and, in 1939, they committed this army to World War II without any consultation. The British Indian Army fought for the United Kingdom in multiple countries: in Ethiopia against the Italian Army; in Egypt, Libya, Tunisia, and Algeria against both the Italian and the German armies; and after Italy surrendered, against the German Army in Italy. A major portion of the Indian Army fought against the Japanese Army, defeating them in Burma. These campaigns cost the lives of more than eighty-seven thousand Indian servicemen, while more than thirty-four thousand were wounded and more than sixty-seven thousand became prisoners of war.[2] Field Marshal Claude Auchinleck, Commander-in-Chief of the Indian Army in 1942, claimed that the British couldn't have gotten through World War I and II if they had not had the Indian Army fighting for them. Winston Churchill also recognized the unsurpassed bravery of these soldiers.[3]

---

[2] Commonwealth War Graves Commission Annual Report 2013-2014.

[3] Bipindra, N.C. *Armed and Ready*. The New India Express, 2013.

Having helped the United Kingdom in winning the war and preserving their freedom, Indians hoped and expected that the British would reward India with its own freedom. But when the war ended, India seemed no closer to independence than it had been at any other time in the twentieth century. This frustrated the political forces in India, including the Indian Congress League, which led the "Quit India" movement, launched by Mahatma Gandhi at the All India Congress Committee session in Bombay on August 8, 1942. One of the most significant points of the resolution was that the movement be non-violent. Immediately after this resolution, Gandhi, the members of the Congress Working Committee, and other Congress leaders were arrested by the British Government. The British also prohibited public assembly. The arrest of Gandhi and the Congress leaders led to mass demonstrations throughout India. Even though the movement had been intended to be non-violent, thousands were killed and injured in its wake. Strikes were called in many places. The British swiftly suppressed many of these demonstrations by mass detentions; more than one hundred thousand people were imprisoned. Most demonstrations were suppressed by 1944, and Gandhi was released from jail. Immediately after his release, Gandhi went on a twenty-one-day hunger strike. Mounting pressure from the rest of the world finally left the British with no choice but to leave India. But the British use of a "Divide and Conquer" strategy would leave a permanent mark on the region.

In order to rule larger populations and forces, the British had used the Roman "Divide et Impera" (Divide and it shall be ours) maxim. In the initial stages of the British rule, the East India Company would incite various kings of smaller states in India to fight among themselves. In the process of such bloody battles, warring kingdoms would become weak, and the British expanded their influence by using the wealth created through trade. Over time, the British used this technique to conquer the entirety of India.

Eventually the British resorted to promoting religious antagonism between the Hindu and Muslim populations as a last attempt to facilitate continued imperial rule. In his book *Inglorious Empire*, Shashi Tharoor, a member of the Indian Parliament, says that what the British did to India "makes a damning case of the British being responsible for systematic destruction of the Indian Society and partition of India which led to the deaths of over a million Indians and displacement of over 17 million families."[4] This was the result of a systematic policy of fomenting hatred between Hindus and Muslims that the British launched to shift the focus of the Indian population to fighting each other rather than fighting the continued effort of the British to occupy India.

[4] Tharoor, Shashi. *Inglorious Empire: What the British Did to India*. Penguin Books, 2018.

For nearly a century, the British had sown the seeds of division within the Indian population. A number of Indian leaders had united Indians under the Congress in 1885. The British, wary of the consequences of this unity, sought to create discord between Hindus and Muslims by preferentially promoting the Muslim minority. To broaden this rift, they introduced the Indian Councils Act of 1909, which established a separate electorate for the Muslim population.[5] The Muslim minority, concerned about the dominance of Hindus, formed the Muslim League. Later, behind the scenes, the British convinced the leader of the Muslim League, Muhammad Ali Jinnah, that Muslims should seek a separate independent state. Jinnah had once been a proponent of collaboration between Hindus and Muslims in India's struggle against British rule. However, when Gandhi unexpectedly captured national and international attention, Jinnah feared that he was losing power. He reinvented himself as the savior of India's Muslims to cement his position as the future head of the Muslim state. Insisting that Muslims and Hindus were two incompatible "nations" living together in one land,[6] he demanded that India be partitioned into two independent states assuring that he would be the premier of the

[5] Burton Stein and David Arnold. *A History of India*. Oxford University Press, 2011.

[6] Khan, Liaquat Ali. *Pakistan, the Heart of Asia*. Sagwan Press, 2015.

nation of Pakistan. In one final push to spare India from the potentially horrendous consequences of Partition, Gandhi offered Jinnah the position of Prime Minister over Jawahar Lal Nehru. However, the talks broke down, and Britain divided India into two nations based upon religion: the Republic of India, populated by the Hindu majority, and the Islamic Republic of Pakistan, populated by the Muslim minority. Pakistan was formed in two dominions: East Pakistan and West Pakistan, separated geographically by India.

*Map of India before the Partition*
Credit: Pre-Partition map of India by mapsofindia.com

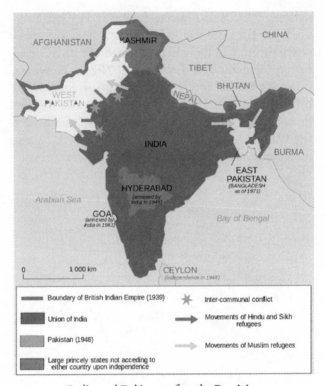

*India and Pakistan after the Partition*
Credit: Map created by Themightyquill via Wikimedia

Hindu families living in the area populated by Muslims had to move to the Hindu majority area, and Muslim families had to migrate to the Muslim majority regions. People used any and every form of transportation to migrate. Many escaped on foot, walking many miles to cross over to their new country. Others used overloaded trains, trucks, or anything that had wheels, including bullock carts or bikes.

*Families escaping from Pakistan to India*
Credit: Photo by Margaret Bourke-White

Many families got separated from each other as people pushed and shoved to get onto the trains. On their way to their new destinations, caravans were intercepted and robbed of their belongings, with Muslim gangs robbing Hindus, and Hindu extremists doing the same to Muslims in revenge.

The Partition of India and Pakistan, a decision made by lawmakers far from the front lines, unleashed an episode of brutal depravity. At least a million people were slaughtered when migrating from their homes to the new nations. Untold numbers of women suffered a fate worse than death, as they were gang-raped, tortured, and then murdered. In many even more tragic cases, fathers, fearing that their daughters would soon be raped (or converted to another faith), pressured and coerced the girls to commit suicide, lest such an event "taint" their family's "honor" and standing in the community. Sometimes, they even killed their female relatives themselves to spare them the shame of rape.

Almost all of the migrants lost everything that they had built over their lifetimes. Our family happened to be Hindus living in the Muslim area and had to migrate to the "new" India. Most of my extended family depended on my father for guidance. Once he knew that we had to leave our home in the middle of the night, he organized everyone to leave together.

I was far too young to remember this. However, my brother Om recalls it well.

"One evening," Om told me, "a group of about a dozen young men marched through the streets of the village chanting slogans like 'Alah-hu-Akbar' (God is Great) and 'Ban-ke-rehega Pakistan' (There will be Pakistan). These were people we knew. They went through the village like a storm, drilling fear through the hearts of all Hindus residing there. Hindu families were stunned. Questions, fears, worries, and uncertainties were ever-apparent on their faces.

"'What is going to happen?' they asked.

"'Will our village fall in Pakistan?'

"'Will our children and females be safe?'

"'Where will we go; what will happen to our homes?'

"Scared out of their wits, Hindu families organized a vigil to protect their families and their belongings.

"'You can't just separate Hindus and Muslims who have been living together for centuries,' many people argued.

"'The political parties can't be that stupid,' they thought aloud.

"The date of the declaration of Independence for India and the creation of a new country for the Muslim population was decided to be the 14th/15th of August. The very next day, the news came that our village, which was a part of the larger area, Lahore Tehsil, had gone to Pakistan.

"Bauji and our uncle Girdhari found out that all the departing Hindu families were meeting at a camp in Kahna Kasha, which was about three miles away from our village. Our extended family entrusted their precious gold with Bauji to get that gold to the meeting place without being robbed. On most days in the morning, he used to go to the land outside the village on a bike to harvest alfalfa for the family water buffaloes. This time, he pretended to do the same, but he collected all the gold in a burlap bag, put a sickle on top, and secured it on the back carrier of his bike. He had traveled a couple of miles outside our village when a group of young Muslim men confronted him, snatched the bag with all the gold jewelry, and disappeared in one of the villages. Our father remembered that he knew one of the residents of the village whose son was one of his students. This man happened to be the *Ziledar* or District Manager. Our father knocked at the Ziledar's door and explained what had transpired. The Ziledar, who was a Muslim, assured my father that he would find the culprits and get the jewelry back. Soon after, the police recovered and returned most of the jewelry to Bauji, who then proceeded to the meeting point with the rest of the relatives."

For a minute, Om closed his eyes as if to thank God for sparing our father. Then he continued.

"All the Hindu families were gathered in the compound of a temple, Arya Samaj Mundir. The temple had high perimeter walls and a big gate. A couple of Dogra Military guards stood at the gate with guns drawn to protect the 'refugees' inside.

"Yes, we had become refugees in our own town, our own homeland, our own country. The camp was crowded. There were so many people in a small area: children crying, women weeping, everyone huddled in the dark with no idea of what the future held for them. The military people were telling everybody to be quiet so as not to attract Muslims with ill-intentions. It was impossible to keep the children quiet. We were all told that it was too risky to continue staying in the camp. We needed to leave for the Indian border right away in the dark. So, long before dawn, all the refugees started their march toward independent India."

The trek from the new territory called "Pakistan" to new "India" was quite fateful for many. The stories I heard remain vivid in my mind, and they are gut-wrenching. Many families were separated from each other, never to be reunited. One of our relatives lost her husband, who was killed by some angry Muslims. She then lost her son, who was separated from her at the train station. Years later, I remember seeing her still crying about her son, trying to locate him fruitlessly in various parts of India.

A caravan of five trucks was lined up at one place ready to take eager families over the border for a steep price. People shoved and pushed their way to get into the trucks. Our extended family was able to board one of these.

*A typical truck in the old days*
Credit: photo by Jacqueline M. Lewis

During the partition time, trucks in India were few and far between. Climbing into the back of a truck was an athletic feat. As our family members did so, Bauji's mother found herself unable to make the climb. After much effort, she gave up and begged her family to leave without her. Bauji refused.

"We will all leave together or die together," he said. "I am not leaving my mother here to be butchered."

Everybody from our extended family got off the truck. The family then decided to proceed to cross the border with a caravan of bullock carts. Later, our family learned that a gang of Muslims had stopped that caravan of trucks, killed all the families, and looted their belongings.

For safety reasons, our bullock cart joined a caravan of other bullock carts loaded with necessities such as food, water, and clothes. Adults walked along the carts and children were loaded on top of the families' meager belongings. It was a thirty-mile trek. A few Indian Army volunteers walked alongside or behind the caravan to protect the caravan from gangs. They had a small cannon mounted on one of the carts. If a gang came toward the caravan, the army would point the cannon at the gang to scare them away. As the caravan crossed the border and we got onto Indian territory, the leader of the Indian Army let out a sigh of relief.

"You were all very lucky that the gangs did not attack," he said. "We had no ammunition in the cannon."

My parents told me, when I was old enough to comprehend, that I was almost a casualty of the Partition. July and August period in India is monsoon season. High temperatures range from the 90's to over 110 degrees in the shade. The travel is made even more miserable by continuous rain for several days at a time and flooding. High temperatures, humidity, water logged fields and dirt roads added to the misery of the caravan going through the fields and dirt roads. As our caravan advanced toward the new Indian border, the dirt road became so muddy that it was impassable for the bullock carts. We had to stop and unload the carts. All the little children, including me, were on the bullock cart. I was sound asleep. One of my uncles unloaded me from the cart and then helped push it through the mud. I found a tree close by and fell asleep hugging it. Once the carts were through the mud, all the little children were lifted back on top of them. My mother believed that my uncle had put me back on and that I was probably asleep on the cart. Unaware of my absence, the caravan proceeded toward the Indian border without me. About a mile later, the caravan stopped for everyone to take a quick drink before continuing the journey. At this point, my mother filled a silver cup with water and decided to wake me for a drink. That's when she discovered that I was not there.

*The silver cup that saved my life...*
Credit: photo by Janet Kumar

Panicked, she asked everybody if they had seen me. At this point, my uncle recalled taking me off the cart but not putting me back on. Like a bolt of lightning, my mother ran toward the spot where the carts had been dismounted. Behind the caravan was the Indian Army protecting the caravan from the gangs. The Pakistani Army was advancing right behind the Indian Army to control the newly established Pakistan territory. The Indian Army that was behind the caravan tried to stop my mother, telling her that they had not seen anybody left behind and that it would be dangerous for her to go back into the Pakistan territory. The Pakistani Army warned that she might not be able to get back to her caravan. Worse yet, the gangs may harm or kill her. But my mother dashed off to find me, followed by my embarrassed uncle. She discovered me hugging a lonely tree and sleeping. Quickly, she snatched me, and made a dash back for the caravan while the Pakistani and Indian armies watched in disbelief. My mother kept the silver cup as a memory of the event, believing the cup had saved my life. Even today, this vessel occupies a prominent space in the Heritage Room in our home in Flower Mound, Texas.

The caravan continued its journey toward the Indian border. The thirty-mile trek took the caravan more than two days to get over to the new border line arbitrarily created by the British. My family tells me that fields along the caravan path were littered with dead bodies and body parts. Open wells and other bodies of water were contaminated with blood and the smell of death. Millions of Hindus and Muslims paid a very dear price for the political ambitions of a few.

Poor, tired, and exhausted from the walk across the newly created borders, our family arrived in the little village of Khalra. Local Hindu families hosted us in a school veranda. We were all seated on a tarp spread on the dirt floor. The local people had cooked simple Indian dishes such as *Dal* and *Roti* (lentil soup and flour tortillas). This was a welcome relief for all the "refugees" who had had nothing to eat for several days.

In 1947, the world-famous photographer, Margaret Bourke-White was sent by *Life* magazine to cover the birth of India and Pakistan. Her pictures published in *Life*, and a few reprinted in Khushwant Singh's famous book *Train to Pakistan*, captured the harrowing accounts of the suffering of people during the Partition. In the words of Khushwant Singh, "The fact is, both sides killed. Both shot and stabbed and speared and clubbed. Both tortured. Both raped. By the summer of 1947, ten million people—Muslims and Hindus and Sikhs—were in flight. Almost a million of them were dead."[7]

Bourke-White herself wrote, "With the coming of Independence to India, the world had the chance to watch a most rare event in the history of nations: the birth of twins—India and Pakistan. It was a birth accompanied by strife and suffering."[8]

This was just the beginning of the journey for my family and me. We moved to a number of villages before settling in Pandori Takhat Mal, abbreviated by us as Pandori or just the *Pind* (village). The total population of the village was around four hundred people with maybe a hundred homes. All the homes, except for one, were constructed of mud and straw. The streets were more like dirt paths. The village had three water ponds and each was full of dirty, contaminated water. Nonetheless, these ponds provided water for our buffaloes and for young kids. We would soak ourselves in the pond water almost every day when it was hot, even though the waters were infested with germs and parasites. People were so poor they could not afford shoes, clothes, or soap. Some of them struggled for food.

7 Singh, Khushwant. *Train to Pakistan*. Penguin Books, 2016.
8 Ibid.

Bauji was a teacher in this village. He was called "the Headmaster" or addressed fondly by the villagers as "*Master ji.*" Later, he also assumed the position of the Postmaster for the village and served on the village elders' council. There were few people who could read or write in Pandori. Therefore, many people asked him to read their letters and write correspondence to their relatives.

Pandori had no running water, so Bauji would tell the villagers when to boil the water before drinking. He applied antiseptics when people hurt themselves. On more than one occasion, I saw him running to see people who had fainted or were having attacks of asthma, diabetes, or epilepsy.

India is divided into four castes: the Brahmins, who belong to the elite caste of teachers; the Kashatris, the warriors; the Vashyas, who farm the land; and the Shudras or the "Untouchables," who work for the farmers and do all the dirty work of cleaning after everybody. Although nobody in our village could be described as rich, the Untouchables were really poor. I saw the Untouchables "sold" for a year for a few hundred rupees. They would work all day in the fields, feed cattle, and clean up after the landowners. They did all this for clothing and food for their families. Young, strong Untouchables fetched up to a thousand rupees and hoped that their children would not be subjected to this if they could save enough money to educate them. I still remember Hindi songs describing the miseries of life.

Some songs asked God why he had abandoned the poor people, while others questioned the sanity of those people who suggested that India was once a great country. Songs such as *"Jinhain naaz tha Hind par voh kahan hain?"* (Where are those people who were proud of India?) expressed the frustrations of a majority of the Indian population.

As I look back at the life in Pandori, it could only be described as a life full of chores and hard work for daily existence. The village had no running water, no electricity, and no paved roads. Almost all homes had no bathroom or toilet facilities inside. Most people got up early in the morning while it was still dark and walked out of the village into the fields to relieve themselves behind bushes and crops. The village had four open wells for common use of the population. A few residents were lucky to have an open well or a handpump in their homes. Almost everybody collected water from the open wells for the daily needs and kept the water in clay vessels. The water was used for bathing, drinking, and washing clothes during the day. Most people kept a water buffalo and a few chickens in the house compound. The water buffalo was a source of milk that was used for drinking, making yogurt, and butter for daily use. As early as 5:00 a.m I could hear women churning butter with a manual churn while the men went out to get alfalfa for feeding the buffaloes. Some people had a small piece of land where they grew crops such as wheat, rice, corn, and sugarcane. They would start working the land with manual tools soon after breakfast. Women were generally at home preparing meals, washing clothes, cleaning the house, and gathering sticks and buffalo chips used as fuel for cooking. The cycle was repeated every single day and life seemed to be a burden. Sad songs written and sung by the poets of the time echoed the sentiment. The closest town was about fourteen miles away, which seemed inaccessible due to lack of transportation.

My father constantly preached the virtue of education. "Education is the only way out of poverty," he would tell anybody who would listen. Many listened to him and to this day remember my father as the man who saved them from the miseries of a life in poverty.

The village had a population of about eighty Untouchables—twenty percent of the total population. They all lived on one side of the village, separated from the rest of us by one street, and only crossing the street to perform their services. Bauji had taught many Untouchable children. He was also on the village elders' council that generally met every evening to review the events of the day. At one of these meetings, he reported that he had been invited to the wedding of one of the Untouchable children. All elders spoke with one voice that Bauji was forbidden to attend the wedding. If he did, he would not be welcome to return to the other side of the street. Bauji did not equivocate for one second, adamantly proclaiming that he would be attending the wedding. In response, the elders followed through on their threat. For many months, they shunned Bauji and barred him from council meetings. But my father was steadfast, and, in time, he won them over and slowly began the process of integration.

It was from this earliest experience that I came to see Bauji as a man whose wisdom extended far beyond that of an ordinary teacher. Bauji's teachings had a powerful effect on my family. All of my siblings acquired advanced degrees. My oldest brother, Om, had a master's degree in two languages and an advanced finance degree. This education enabled him to eventually become a general manager of a global company, Singer Machines of India. My elder sister, Pushpa, finished her high school and associate degree in Hindi and married a doctor. My second brother, Dwarka, finished his civil engineering degree and worked in various positions in India and Iraq building irrigation systems in those countries. My younger sister, Usha, finished her MS in chemistry and worked in the Indian School systems, advancing from a teacher's position to principal of a highly acclaimed college. I finished my undergraduate degree in dairy technology in India, followed by a MS and PhD in food science and nutrition from The Ohio State University, and an MBA from the University of Chicago, with a major concentration in international finance and marketing.

Many other people from the little village of Pandori who were educated by Bauji have also done well. A friend of mine, Kashmir Lal, recently retired from a prestigious position in the state of Punjab. Another young child tutored by Bauji, Gurcharan Singh Randhawa, is a prominent doctor in Marshalltown, Iowa.

Bauji's day in Pandori started at 4 a.m. After his morning walk of two miles or so, he would feed and milk our buffalo. This routine was followed by a full day of work. He would end the day by feeding and milking the buffalo again before meeting with the village elders. His workday was usually sixteen hours, and he instilled that work ethic in all his children.

By the time of his retirement, Bauji had made the village of Pandori a much better place than it was when he first arrived. The testimonial to his contributions is apparent in the way that the people of that village have remembered him. My son Daven and I visited Pandori in 2007, almost fifty years after our family had left it. When we got there, an old lady in the street approached us.

"You are Kanshi Ram's son, aren't you?" she asked me. When I nodded in the affirmative, she gave me a hug. "Your father was a saint, you know. He helped us all a lot. We miss him so much."

Both Daven and I were struck by the lasting impact one person can have for generations. Many years after meeting that woman in Pandori, I came to realize that the reason my father's teachings affected that village in such a sustainable way was that they were truly universal lessons. I made it my mission to distill his lessons down to their essence, and what I came away with was sixteen principles.

1. You and you alone are the architect of your destiny.
2. Choose to be a victor, not a victim.
3. Be happy in your situation until you can change the situation.
4. Money is good only if it does any good.
5. Nothing great was ever built on a weak foundation.
6. Whatever you want to achieve, give it your all.
7. Set high goals and work hard to achieve them.
8. Education is the only way out of poverty.
9. You must make the tough choices to be successful in life.
10. Live your life by your own design, principles, and values.

11. Focus on what is really important to achieve your goals.
12. Never forget where you came from.
13. Wherever you go, leave the place better than you found it.
14. Encourage your children to fly as high as they can.
15. Do your best; the universe will do the rest.
16. Hard work is the only path to your desired destination.

I believe these principles have relevance to anyone's life. The effect they have had for decades on the people in a tiny village in India is the same effect they can have on you, regardless of your circumstances or where you live. In this book, I am going to examine each of these principles through the lens of how it affected me or a member of my family. By doing this, my goal is to provide you with the tools you need to apply these principles to your own life.

In this way, the lessons of Bauji will live to touch future generations. I can think of no better tribute to him.

And I can think of no better teacher for you.

Let's begin.

# Principle #1:
# You and You Alone Are the
# Architect of Your Destiny

The year was 1959 and at the young age of fifteen, I finished high school. Education in India had been at that point (and still is) highly competitive. High school final exams are conducted on a national basis. With very few colleges in the country, every student participating in these exams was competing for a limited number of entry positions in prestigious universities. The final exams consisted of taking three-hour tests in eight subjects within one week in a centralized location chosen by the government. The test questions were kept confidential to avoid any cheating. These tests were tough and nerve-wracking, and every student prepared for months before sitting for these exams. Every student's future was riding on their results on these finals.

I was studying at the DAV High School in Amritsar, India. This school happened to be one of the best and most prestigious, and there were many brilliant students taking the finals along with me. About a month after the exams every year, the results of these finals were published in the state and the national newspapers. Only about 10-15 percent of the high school graduates would be selected for college education. At such a young age, the pressure of getting grades to qualify for entrance in a good college or university was almost unbearable for me and all the friends I knew. Soon thereafter would come the reports of students committing suicide after learning that they had failed to get high grades.

With the stakes so high and my competition so evident all around me, I was feeling considerable pressure to succeed. And once I finished taking the tests, I felt completely drained by the entire experience. I had returned home to Pandori, but the exams stuck with me. I kept going over the test questions in my mind and second-guessing my answers. I was uncertain, anxious, and very concerned about my future.

One morning, when Bauji and I were walking to the alfalfa fields to harvest the feed for our buffalo, he asked me how I thought I did on my finals. The anxiety and stress I felt while I waited for my results boiled over. Raising my voice—which I never did with him—I said, "Bauji, I really don't know, and I don't care. I do not plan to go to college anyway. I am tired of studying! I have no life!"

Bauji was stunned. He had never heard me speak so heatedly. For a moment, he was speechless, but he soon gathered himself. He stopped in the middle of his walk, turned to me, and said, "*Beta* (son), this is your life. You and you alone are the architect of your life. I am here as your coach, your guide. Of course, the decision to go to college or not is yours. In deciding your future path, ask yourself a question, though: 'If college is not on my life path, then what is my destination?'"

I remember feeling a lump in my throat. I had no idea of my life destination. Who and what would I be when I grew up? The images of some of the young people in the village who worked all day in the fields for landowners flashed through my mind. I imagined darkness in my future as far as I could see. A trickle of tears slowly rolled down my face and onto the dust of our walking path. We both walked silently for about fifteen minutes before I could finally speak.

"I am so sorry, Bauji," I said at last. "I'm stressed and confused and not thinking straight. I will take this time to think about my life. I will decide my life purpose and destination. I know that education is the only way for any of us to prosper. I am just frustrated that I don't know the results of my finals and I do not know whether I will make the cut to be able to go to a good college. Please forgive me for my outburst."

Since I've already given you some of my background, you know that my test scores were good enough to land me in a prestigious university, which took me to the postgraduate degrees that put me on my professional path. My life destination, which was in truth already clear to me even before my outburst with Bauji, became much clearer as my education progressed, and I set off on a course that has afforded me an enormous amount of career and personal satisfaction. But the key lesson that Bauji delivered during this fateful conversation was one that has proven invaluable to me over the years: that my destiny is firmly in my hands. I am responsible for the decisions I make and, while I might seek the counsel of others, I alone am to credit or blame for how things turn out in my life. That day, I learned that I needed to be the architect of my own life because my life was too important to be left to other people's designs.

This lesson from Bauji is first in this book because it is fundamental to all of the other lessons I will be sharing with you. If you are truly going to be able to enhance your place in the world, you need to accept that this is all going to be the result of the decisions *you* make. Yes, outside forces might have an effect on how things turn out for you, but you alone choose how you will react to every condition in which you find yourself. If you don't accept this fact, you will forever believe that others determine your fate, and you will be relinquishing power that no human being should ever surrender.

So, how do you incorporate this lesson into your life in such a way that this mindset becomes second nature? I recommend that you start every day with an action plan. Ask yourself what you want to accomplish that day to move closer to your goals, and then take the actions necessary to accomplish them. This will serve you well both in the short term and the long term. In the short term, you will make a habit of setting an agenda for yourself that includes making palpable progress. And in the long term, you will be reinforcing your role in your own destiny and begin living the reality that no one other than you is in charge of what you make of yourself.

# Exercise 1: Create a plan for living your life by design

The life you are living today was created by your own vision and design, or you were guided by somebody else such as your parents or other influencers in your life. It is also possible that you just drifted to your current state without any design. The probability of achieving your life goals is significantly higher if you have a clear idea of what those goals are. As Lewis Carroll articulated, "If you don't know where you are going, any road will get you there." With a clear destination and goals to get there, all of your senses become focused and, surprisingly, the universe seems to help. In the words of Paulo Coelho, "If you want something in life, the whole universe will conspire to make it happen." In order to develop your plan, it is important that:

- You know yourself.
- You know what you want your life to be.
- You know your goals.
- You have clear action plans.
- You execute your plans with discipline, while learning and improving as necessary.

The following guide is designed to help you be clear about designing and achieving your life plan.

The best way to create a plan is to start writing down answers to the questions below. Do not worry about being perfect; just start. You will have many opportunities to modify the plan. For now, just let your mind flow.

I. *Who am I?*

This is the toughest question. It calls for introspection, and is intended to help you understand your values, your passions and interests, and even the areas that you want to avoid.

Carve out a two-hour block of your time. Find a quiet place away from your daily routine. Calm your mind by taking a few deep breaths. In key inspiring phrases, start writing:

I am:

-------------------------------------------
-------------------------------------------
-------------------------------------------
-------------------------------------------
-------------------------------------------
-------------------------------------------

## II. *What is my ideal life?*

Create a set of phrases that describe your ideal life.

------------------------------------------------

------------------------------------------------

------------------------------------------------

------------------------------------------------

------------------------------------------------

## III. *What are my key goals?*

Select three to five major things you want to accomplish. For a more detailed plan, you can give your goals categories, such as "Personal Goals," "Professional Goals," "Family Goals," "Financial Goals," and so on.

------------------------------------------------

------------------------------------------------

------------------------------------------------

------------------------------------------------

## IV. *What are my action plans?*

For each category of your goals, develop a set of actions and establish the timetable necessary for these actions. For example:

*Action Plans for my professional goals:*

What are my current realities (my current profession)?

_____
_____

What is my ideal profession/job?

_____
_____

Where do I want to be in five years?

_____
_____

What is my One-year Plan? (Specific "To Do" by Month/Week)

_____
_____

*V. Disciplined Follow-through*

Keep a journal of:
  • The progress you made toward your goals last week.

- What you want to accomplish in the coming week.
- Specific actions you need to take.
- People you need to enroll to help you (a coach, a network of supporters, a personal advisory board, &c.).

It is important to have a network of people to help keep you on your path. Often you can find these people from your contacts and create an arrangement where you offer each other help in development. A coach can help you improve your skills and approaches. Your network of supporters is generally composed of your friends, family members, and coworkers. They can help you build additional contacts and resources from their own contacts. A "Personal Advisory Board" is akin to advisory boards that business CEOs use to seek council and advice on different subjects to help advance their business. Your personal advisory board consists of people from your professional contacts who have expertise in different areas of your personal and professional interests. They can advise you informally on how to use different approaches to achieve your goals. By sharing your expertise with them, you can get the board members without monetary compensation. Just ask. Most good people are keen to help.

# Principle #2:
# Choose to Be a Victor, Not a Victim

As a young boy, whenever I read history books, I was inspired by the people who changed the course of humankind or lived by their principles for the good of others or invented something that made a difference in the lives of people. During my junior year in high school, I read a history book of the British Raj. One of the stories that had an impact on me was that of Lord Robert Clive, who became the Commander-in-Chief of British India. I was mesmerized by the accomplishments of a man who had at one point in his youth tried to commit suicide by putting a pistol to his head and trying to shoot himself three times. When the pistol misfired all three times, Clive decided that his life must have been spared because he was supposed to accomplish something big with it. And indeed he did. Clive started his career as a member of the East India Company. But he would go on to help found the British Raj, lead British India, and become one of the wealthiest people in the world.

Of course, he did this on the backs of an enormous number of people. Clive was one of the architects of the divide-and-conquer approach to conquering India that I mentioned earlier. The British claimed that they did a great deal for India—they built the railway infrastructure and roads, built schools, provided financial resources, and moved the country into the twentieth century in many other ways. But there was another side to this. Indians who lived under the British rule accused the British of looting Indian resources, using Indian soldiers to preserve their kingdom during the World Wars, and discriminated against Indians on their own land. History shows that this caused the divisions within India that ultimately led to the Partition.

I was too young to remember life under British rule, but the more I learned about it the more I felt I needed to understand what conditions were truly like. I decided to ask Bauji during one of our walks. He stopped in his tracks as if to collect the words for exactly what he wanted to convey.

"It depends on who you ask," he replied at last. "A lot of people felt like they were slaves of the British. Others enjoyed working for them, and many others just went with the flow."

"How about you Bauji? How did you feel?"

"Some of the British treated us like slaves. However, I decided that I would never feel that way."

Bauji then proceeded to tell me about an encounter that he'd had with the British Army.

"I was about fourteen years old at the time. I happened to be in Lahore to run errands. While I was there, a small contingent of the British Army marched through the streets of the city. Whenever the British Army marched through towns, all Indians were supposed to line the streets and salute the soldiers as they marched by. I was standing with a number of other people and, when the army passed, I did not salute. Frankly, I had no idea that I was supposed to do that. As the soldiers got to where I was standing, the commander saw me. He pulled me out of the line and beat me with his baton for not saluting."

I was stunned to hear this. No one had ever mentioned this incident to me before.

"Don't you hate the British for that?" I said.

Bauji replied calmly. "No, I do not. One man does not represent the nation, and if I hate him or the British, I would be turning myself into a victim. And if I did that, none of the people who did me wrong would wind up being punished, anyway. The only person who would be punished would be me, because I would be punishing myself by being angry." Then Bauji repeated the advice of Buddha in our language. Remember, he said, *"You will not be punished for your anger; you will be punished by your anger. To be angry is to let the mistakes of others punish you. Holding on to anger is like grasping a hot coal with the intent of throwing it at someone else; you are the one who gets burned.*

"Instead, it's important to use experiences like this to do more with your life. In many ways, this is the story of India. What that commander did to me is an example of the kind of behavior that led to the end of the British Raj. Remember the 'Quit India' movement started when some Britishers threw Gandhi off a train because he was an Indian and was not allowed to travel in the first-class compartment."

Bauji was of course right. If he'd let anger fester over what had happened to him, he would have let his sense of victimhood define him. Instead, he chose to use this experience as inspiration for living a life of commitment to helping others lift themselves up.

Bauji is right that this story was representative of the entire nation of India. I have watched the progress of the country over the seventy-five years since the nation got its independence. The progress of India and Indians living abroad is nothing short of miraculous. Since independence, India has transformed the education, transportation, communication, and banking systems. Here are a few examples of the transformation:

• Food Production: Right after independence, basic commodities such as wheat and sugar were in critical shortage. I remember lining up for hours to collect our rationed quantities of food. India depended upon international food aid up to the mid-1960s. Today, India is self-sufficient in food production and exports various food grains. India is now the largest producer of fresh fruits, milk, pulses and oil seeds, and sun-

flower seeds and the second-largest producer of wheat, rice, sugarcane, potatoes, tea,
and cotton in the world.

• Life Expectancy: In 1947, the average life
expectancy was only 32 years. Seventy years
later, life expectancy is 69. Major epidemics
such as plague, polio, and malaria have been
eradicated.

• Literacy: The literacy rate in India in
1947 was 12%. Since then it has grown to
74%.

• Advanced Education: The number of
universities grew from 20 to more than 700
between 1947 and 2015. The number of colleges grew from 496 to almost 40,000. Nearly 27 million students were enrolled in Indian graduate programs in 2015 with 9 million
graduating. India has developed into one of
the largest exporters of talent to other parts
of the world in the fields of IT, medicine,
and engineering.

• Standard of Living: GDP growth of India is among the top five countries in the
world, and the standard of living has con-
sistently improved since independence.

This transformation has been especially evident
in the United States. A number of years ago, I was
heading Research and Development for Warner
Lambert, a pharmaceutical company. At an event,

I shared the stage with a Finnish executive from Nokia, and we spoke afterward.

"I visited New York in 1966," he told me. "I saw Indians driving taxicabs, running small motels, and owning a few gas stations. I thought that was their niche in the US. Here I am thirty years later, and I see Indians in leadership positions in IT, consumer product companies, and in the medical field. What a transformation."

To me, this enormous evolution comes directly from the Indian response to independence. Though independence came with an enormous set of challenges, it also freed Indians to show what they were made of. Indians did not look at themselves as victims. They chose to look forward to leveraging the freedom from the British Raj to educate themselves and to compete on the world stage in IT, medicine, finance, technology, and science. Indians did not ask the British to compensate India or her people for all the gold, jewels, and other assets and natural resources the British took from them. Instead, they focused their energies on creating a future for themselves and for their children where no one would take from them again.

Most of us can point to some experience in our lives or maybe even an entire component of our lives where we have been victimized. However, the wrongs done to us do not need to define us. Instead, they can serve as the foundation for transforming ourselves into victors. Just as so many Indians took their adverse conditions as motivation for freeing themselves from these conditions, you can do the same thing with the ways in which you have been wronged. Use the pain you feel as a guide to taking you to the exact opposite feeling. In doing so, you will avoid being a victim and instead become a victor.

## Exercise 2: Transform from victim to victor

Transformation starts with our thoughts. In the words of the ancient Chinese philosopher, Lao Tzu:

> Watch your thoughts, they become words;
> Watch your words, they become actions;
> Watch your actions, they become habits;
> Watch your habits, they become character;
> Watch your character, for it becomes your destiny.

In effect, the difference between being a victim and a victor is determined by the difference in your thoughts and beliefs. Here are some thoughts and actions to help you develop a victor mindset.

*I. Start your day with positive thoughts.*

Before you begin your day, take 15-20 minutes of your time for breathing exercises or meditation to center yourself. Follow this by repeating the following affirmations:

- I am choosing to change my thoughts and behaviors to be a victor and not a victim of my circumstances or other people's behaviors.
- I choose to align my actions with my thoughts of being a victor.
- I know my life goals, and I know I will achieve my goals.
- I am choosing to live my life by my own values.
- I choose not to be afraid of others or of making mistakes. I will learn from my encounters and mistakes.

*II. Enable and empower yourself with good health. Exercise 30-60 minutes daily.*

*III. Surround yourself with positive people (Energizers). Avoid negative thoughts and people (Energy Drainers).*

*IV. At the end of the day, record what energized you and what you learned.*

# Principle #3:
# Be Happy in Your Situation Until You Can Change the Situation

I do not recall Bauji ever complaining about anything. If something was not to his liking, he either changed it or he accepted it. My mother, Bhabiji, was often traveling, sometimes to take one of the children to a doctor (which, even if she was just going to the nearest town, took the entire day) or to be with my sister Pushpa, helping her before and after the birth of her children. Bhabiji was a good cook. Unfortunately, her children did not inherit that talent from her. Pushpa recalls an occasion when both Bhabiji and Bauji were away for the day. That meant that preparing dinner was left to her and my brother Om. Pushpa cooked Indian lentil soup and, when she tasted it, discovered that the soup was excessively salty. She sought Om's advice on this problem. Om suggested that they add sugar to the soup to mask the taste of salt. Any chef would cringe at the very idea, but Pushpa and Om proceeded to continue adding sugar and tasting the soup until they ran out of sugar. Bauji got home and Pushpa served the soup, anxiously waiting for our father's reaction.

"That is quite a novel soup recipe," was all he said. He then finished the bowl without showing any sign of disapproval, even though the meal must have been dreadful. The circumstances had presented him with an awful dinner and, since he didn't have the power to change the circumstances on that night, he chose to be happy with it.

Not only did Bauji refuse to complain, but he had a hard time listening to his children complain about their situations. "If you are unhappy, do something about it," he would say. While all of us had learned not to complain about whatever was happening in our lives, we would slip once in a while. One such encounter drove Bauji's message home for me, though.

I had joined the National Dairy Research Institute (NDRI) in Karnal. I was seventeen years old and the first year of Technical College was hard on nearly all the students who were in my class. The coursework was tough. We attended classes six days a week from 8:00 a.m. to 5:00 p.m., followed by physical training for an hour. After doing our homework assignments including taking care of the animals, all students went to the mess hall for dinner. All of us were required to be in our formal school clothes until 10:00 p.m.

We were living in dorms, away from our homes. The dorms were in an isolated area about three miles from the nearest town. The 3200-acre campus was fenced in with a barbed wire, and students were only allowed to go to town once a week on Saturday for three hours. At the time, it felt like being in a prison. More than half of the 45 first-year students quit and went back to their homes within the first three months. I myself was at a breaking point and was seriously considering leaving NDRI, giving up on the enormous opportunity that I'd received by being admitted to the school.

During the first six months of classes, we were allowed four days of vacation to visit home. Bauji was still teaching, but he had been transferred to At-ari, a village about twenty-five miles away from our home in Pandori. Bhabiji was still living in Pandori and taking care of my younger sister, Usha. Bhabiji would keep herself busy. She would spin cotton into yarn and then weave blankets that we used for our beds. She would sew our clothes. Because we did not have much money, every week she would trek three miles to collect cotton from the nearby village, spin it all week, and then take the yarn back. All of this work would fetch her two rupees, which at the time was equal to about twenty cents—today it would be equal to three cents. Neither of my parents had easy lives but, true to form, you would never know how challenging their situations were by talking to them.

During my break, I went to visit Bauji in Atari, in the tiny room at which he was staying. Bauji looked frail. Living away from home was clearly having an effect on him. He did not know how to cook (a likely source of his frailty), but he wanted to make sure that both of us got something to eat. My eyes still well up when I remember how difficult it was for him to build a fire with cow dung patties from scratch during monsoon season and then cook us a rice dish (Khichri) that looked like risotto. Quietly we ate our humble meals.

"How are you doing, Bauji?" I said while we ate. He raised his head from his plate.

"I have my son with me, and my family is safe and working hard to get their educations. We are healthy, and we have food. What more can a father ask for?"

He reached over and gently kissed my forehead. At that point, he seemingly realized that he'd shown too much affection to be able to retain his image of a disciplinarian, so he picked up his plate and motioned me to follow.

"Let's go now," he said. "We have a lot to talk about. Tell me how you are doing in college."

Given what I'd been considering, this was a loaded question. But having seen what he was going through without complaint, I knew there was only one answer to it.

"I am doing well, Bauji," I said softly.

Yes, college had been a very difficult adjustment for me and, yes, I had been feeling so much discomfort with the situation that I'd considered giving up. But how could I complain about such things when my father was dealing with a much greater challenge with a smile?

That day with my father would change my life forever. My education at NDRI has been a key source of my professional success and personal friendships. After graduating from NDRI, I got a job with Hindustan Lever, a subsidiary of Unilever where I met Dr. Ashok Ganguly. Dr. Ganguly urged and inspired me to explore educational opportunities in the United States. I completed my PhD at The Ohio State University, and multiple career opportunities followed over the years. I still have exceptionally strong relationships with my college friends from NDRI and have found great friends in the US. If not for that day with my father, I do not know if I would have had such a fulfilling personal and professional life.

The problem with complaining about any tough situation you might be enduring is that it's too easy to make the complaint itself your only action. It is important to take stock of your life on a regular basis and to make an honest appraisal of what is working and what is not. However, complaining about the things that are not working is not productive in any way. If you are in a position to change these things immediately, do so. If you are not, don't allow your displeasure with these things to darken the rest of your life. Accept them for what they are until you can change them.

# Exercise 3: Create a plan for positive change

In the book, *Riding the Blue Train*, that I co-authored with my friend, Bart Sayle, we provided a framework for assessing one's current situation and to develop a plan for change. The key questions are:

- What is working for me?
- What is not working for me?
- What is possible for me?
- What is missing which I need to add, fix, or change?

Once you have assessed the situation you are currently in, create a future state for yourself and a plan for positive change. Be persistent and follow your action plan for change. In the meantime, do not focus on what is not working. Focus your energy on the positive changes you are making.

# Principle #4:
# Money Is Good Only If It Does Any Good

Life after the Partition was full of uncertainties. Nearly all the refugees who had migrated from Pakistan to India had very few worldly possessions left. Meanwhile, there was a near-catastrophic shortage of life-supporting essentials such as food, fuel, and clothing on a nationwide level. Even if you had money, finding the basic necessities of life in the rural areas was challenging. In this environment of shortages, poor transportation systems, and political chaos, most people were uncertain about where their next meal would come from. Our family was no different—except for the empowering beliefs of Bauji.

"With independence comes the responsibility of self-dependence. We will need to be self-sufficient and self-supporting to deserve our independence. As long as we are dependent on government systems, we are not truly independent. We must rebuild our lives and emerge even stronger, financially and spiritually. Then we will be independent permanently."

Considering the bleak outlook for the country at the time, this was a bold sentiment. Financial systems and institutions in India were in complete disarray. There were a few banks in large cities such as Delhi, Bombay (now Mumbai), Calcutta (now Kolkata), and Madras (now Chennai). Rural areas, where more than seventy percent of the population lived, had no access to banks or any other financial institutions where people could deposit or borrow money.

Rakesh Mohan, a Senior Fellow at the Jackson Institute for Global Affairs at Yale University, has traced the history of the Indian financial sector after independence. According to Mohan, "At the time of independence in 1947, India had 97 scheduled private banks, 557 'non-scheduled' (small) private banks organized as joint stock companies, and 395 cooperative banks. The decades of 1950s and 1960s were characterized by limited access to finance of the productive sector and a large number of banking failures."[9]

With the lack of banking institutions and no access to government programs similar to Social Security or Welfare, people depended on friends, acquaintances, and family for funds during difficult economic times. Absent such help, poor people fell prey to loan sharks who charged prohibitively high interest rates, driving people into a deeper cycle of poverty.

Bauji saw the devastating effects of this vicious cycle and made a rule for the family.

"We will save half of what we make every month for the 'rainy season,'" he said.

---

[9] Mohan, Rakesh; Indian Financial Sector: Structure, Trends and Turns, *IMF Working Paper No. 17/7* 2017.

The rule was simple. Living with that rule, however, was anything but. All of our financial resources would go toward the basic needs of the family: food, shelter, and clothing. This meant getting by with little more than subsistence. Food consisted of chapati or rice, yogurt, lentils, or pickles, and fresh vegetables when available. Shelter was a mud home given to our father by the village in return for his teaching services. Clothing consisted of two sets of cotton clothes for everybody in the family—one to wear and the other for use when the first set was being washed. For the children in the family, education was the only other priority. By focusing on these simple needs of life, Bauji was able to save half of his monthly income. The savings were to be used later for higher education, emergencies, and other needs such as weddings.

Amazingly, I do not recall missing anything. As a matter of fact, the rule helped all of us build close relationships within and outside of the family. We all learned to be creative in finding ways to entertain ourselves and to build or fix household things.

Most of our relatives were pretty much in financial ruin after the Partition. Some families had been able to escape with the cash and some gold they grabbed as they ran from their homes in Pakistan. Most of them tried starting small businesses to make a living when they got to their new homes. But after a few months, most of our relatives abandoned their businesses to preserve the little capital they had.

Indian families generally have close-knit relationships. Since most of the people have gone through tough economic times, extended family members help each other whenever they can. This custom helped our family to survive during the post-Partition days. People shared food, clothing, and all other necessities. A few months after the Partition, Bauji was fortunate to get a teaching job with the state government of Punjab. The salary was quite low, but Bauji found ways to save some of the money he earned by bartering tutoring services for food and other necessities.

Among our many relatives was Harbans Lal, a man we knew as our uncle even though he was Bauji's cousin. Harbans was an affable young man, and he'd started a grocery shop in one of the villages. Unfortunately, the business was unsuccessful. Harbans lost the little capital he had to the point that he could not even afford food for his family. A proud man by nature, Harbans had no choice but to look for a loan. With the lack of established banking and financial systems, and without any collateral to get a loan from the village loan sharks, Harbans approached Bauji.

"I have nothing to offer as a collateral," he said to my father. "I don't even have a good track record of running a business. I can assure you, though, that I have learned a lot from the last business, and I think I can make the next business successful. What you have is my word that I will work very hard and I will do everything possible to pay back the loan. I know that we are all strapped for cash, but if you have any to lend me, my family and I will be eternally grateful to you."

He sat back and waited for a response from Bauji.

"I know you, and I trust you," my father said. "You are right. We are all strapped for cash. However, I know you need the money more than I do right now. After all, what is the money good for if it is not used to do some good? At this time, any money I have is yours, because it will do the most good if you can use that money to rebuild your business and your life. I am not worried about getting it back. When you are successful, I know you will help other family members who may be in need."

Bauji went into his room and brought back a handkerchief that contained all of his savings, handing this money over to Harbans.

Harbans took that money and invested in his new business. This time, the business became quite successful and he thrived. He never forgot the kindness, the generosity, and the trust placed in him by Bauji. Our families became very close, and Harbans expressed his gratitude to Bauji every chance he got. Of course, he paid back the loan. He also helped other members of our extended family whenever he could.

I benefited directly from this principle of Bauji's. After graduation from college at the age of nineteen, I secured a job. After working for a couple of years, I decided to pursue an advanced education in the United States. I had saved some money, but not enough to pay my airfare. When the time came to leave India, I approached Bauji for the money I needed for airfare and other expenses. Without hesitation, he brought out his savings book, opened the book, and said, "This is all the money we have. Let me know how much you need, and I will withdraw it tomorrow." I was upset to realize that I needed nearly all of it. Bauji had just retired, which meant that my parents needed that money to live. However, the next day, he withdrew most of his money and gave it to me.

"This will help you fulfill your dream of completing your PhD," he said. "We will find a way to do without it."

I got to The Ohio State University in 1966 to work on my PhD. Bauji never asked me to pay him back. However, not for a single day did I forget my parents' sacrifice. I became a research assistant at the university, making $250 per month out of which I paid taxes, rent, my living expenses, and my education expenses. However, as soon as I would get my paycheck, I would send $25 (200 rupees) every month to my parents.

This principle has become such a part of my life that my wife Janet and I have helped four of our nephews through college in the United States without expecting anything in return. Janet and I also helped her family financially whenever any of them needed it. One such event was when we got a call from Janet's mom at 2:00 a.m.. Janet's father, who was a farmer, had borrowed money from the bank. The loan was to be paid back when the crops came in. However, that season's soybean crop was partially destroyed by floods. The loan was due, and Janet's father could not cover the loan. Being a proud man, he would not ask for help and would have lost the farm to the bank. Janet's mom could not sleep. She called us to see if we could help. Both Janet and I, without any hesitation, withdrew every last penny we had saved and gave it to her parents to save their farm from foreclosure. We have also started a charitable foundation in the name of Bauji that supports students who need financial help to complete their education and other people who need help with their medical expenses. With the assistance of the Wm. Wrigley Jr. Company, we also funded a scholarship program for as many as four students at my alma mater, the National Dairy Research Institute in India.

We all know how important money is to our everyday lives. And for many people, there's rarely enough to make ends meet. However, it is often the case that what we see as "essential" is instead a luxury in disguise. Bauji used to classify spending as (a) absolutely essential; (b) would like to have; and (c) luxury. The only expenses that met his criteria for "absolutely essential" were:

- Food: Simple, minimal food sufficient for survival.
- Clothing: Two sets of simple clothes made at home.
- Education

Neither I nor any of my siblings had a pair of shoes until the age of ten. One time, when I was in the eighth grade, I asked Bauji for a penny as I was leaving for school in the morning.

"What do you need the money for?" he asked.

Sheepishly, I explained that I wanted to buy some lunch.

"Did your mother pack you a lunch?" he countered.

"Yes Bauji. But it is the same tortilla and pickle every day. I would like to buy lunch today, just like all my classmates."

"Sorry, you will have to eat what your mother packed for you. I have money only for necessities."

What Bauji taught me, and what has become a fundamental part of my life, is that it is important to create financial independence for yourself and that you must prioritize how you spend. Whenever you are using the rest of your money for good, you are doing something priceless.

## Exercise 4: Develop a financial plan and stick to it

One of the lessons I have learned during my business career is that your chances of success are high if you are absolutely clear about the outcomes you want to achieve, know your current situation, and then develop the strategy and plan to accomplish your desired outcomes. In order to help others financially, the first step is to be financially secure yourself.

*I. Financial security for yourself and your family:*

Unless you were born with a silver spoon or won a lottery, the common steps are:
- Become financially knowledgeable.
- Write your financial goals.
- Build a budget.
- Save a portion of your income.
- Have a plan for paying off your debt.
- Invest to grow your wealth.

You can develop a plan by reading a financial planning book and/or consulting with a credible professional.

## II. *Doing good for others:*

Until you have become financially secure, you can do something good for others by sharing non-monetary assets such as your time and advice. Once you feel good about your own finances, you can help others financially as well. Again, know the outcomes you want to achieve (your philanthropic goals). For example, you may want to help students in need of financial help to complete their education or you may want to help people who cannot work due to physical or mental illness. The choice for charitable giving is yours. Know how you would measure the effectiveness of your generosity.

# Principle #5: Nothing Great Was Ever Built on a Weak Foundation

As a father and as a teacher, Bauji believed that the values and habits of children are established at a very early age. He emphasized, "If you start at childhood with good values and principles, they become your life-long habits and practices. The same is true if you are exposed to bad values and habits.

"Childhood is the time when you build a strong set of values, principles, and habits," he would tell his children and his pupils. "They are the foundation of a great life. Remember, nothing great—including buildings, societies, kingdoms, or countries—was ever built on a weak foundation."

I have no idea where or how he developed this belief system, but he lived it every day of his life.

He supported his words with actions. He believed that the pillars of a strong foundation for human beings consisted of a set of good human values, a sound education, single-minded focus, hard work, good nutrition, a vigorous exercise regimen, responsible financial management, and a simple life. He also believed that parents and teachers can only influence children by becoming an example. In our family, my oldest brother, Om, was the first child who saw Bauji live his principles.

"Even before the Partition when we were in Pakistan, Bauji would wake up at 4:00a.m. and then wake me up. He would massage our bodies with mustard oil, and we would do a few stretching exercises. We both would then go for a run along the bank of an irrigation canal. We would run at least two miles. That was our daily exercise regimen. Our diet was very basic. After a simple breakfast, I went to school. Bauji was a teacher there. The day was filled with an intense study program. Bauji expected nothing less than the best effort from all his students. At the end of each day, all students recited addition and multiplication tables. All Bauji's students became exceptionally good in math. We did our homework after school, then we did our household chores. Sometimes, I got a few minutes of playing time with my friends before dinner. After we ate, several students would come over to our home, and Bauji would tutor all of us until late in the evening."

This might sound like a tough daily schedule for an eight-year old child, but Bauji was convinced that allowing his children to be lax early in their lives would lead to their underachieving later. Given the success my brother has had in his life, it's difficult to argue with the effectiveness of Bauji's plan. I personally went through a similar disciplined daily life in my early childhood, and so did many other students of Bauji. He tutored them all at no cost to them. Many of those children grew up to be very successful in their careers. Even today, those students credit Bauji for their successes. And they have passed these lessons on to their children by instilling the good values and principles that made them successful.

Whatever I have become as a man or have achieved in my professional career, the foundation of that was laid a long time ago during my early years of childhood.

## The Foundation of Education

Bauji was singularly focused on ensuring that his children got a good education. His mantra was, "Education is one of the key pillars on which you build a successful life." He never wavered from his commitment to education and he made sure that each of his children got an advanced education at a time in India when only a small percentage of the population was even literate. Indeed, education has been the key to my success in life. My education paved the way for my rewarding career at world-class food and pharmaceutical companies, including Unilever, Quaker Oats, Frito Lay, PepsiCo, Warner Lambert, Bristol Myers Squibb, and the Wm. Wrigley Jr. Company. Just as rewarding has been the personal growth from being able to work with professionals all over the globe. It all started with Bauji's belief in the value of education.

## The Foundation of Hard Work

As the headmaster of the only elementary school in our village of Pandori, Bauji was my father and my teacher. Bauji instilled the value of hard work—at home and at school—from my early childhood, and this has served me well in my education and in my career. As far back as I can remember, my daily schedule began with very early morning walks with Bauji, walking more than a mile to harvest alfalfa for our buffalo, cutting the alfalfa into bite-size pieces, and feeding the buffalo. My day continued with getting ready for school, doing projects with my mother at home, and, after dinner, studying in the dim light of a kerosene lamp late into the night with other students of Bauji.

At the age of seven, I recall working with my mother to build a mud wall around the compound of our home. Bhabiji would use an old shovel to dig a big hole in the middle of the compound. The clay from the hole was then mixed with water and wheat straw. My mother and I then would knead the clay by constantly stomping in the mud and picking out any little rocks. The clay eventually became more like a dough. Mom would then pack the clay in a wooden mold about twelve inches long and eight inches wide. The clay was allowed to dry overnight until the mold could be removed without deforming the "brick," after which she used the mold for the next mud brick. It took several days for the clay bricks to dry completely after that. We used those bricks to build the basic frame of the wall using wet clay as the mortar between the bricks. Once the basic structure of the wall was constructed with the clay/mud bricks, she allowed the entire wall to dry for several days. My mother then combined chopped-up wheat straw with mud and cow and/or buffalo dung to make a paste that served as the plaster over the entire wall.

## The Foundation of Focus

Bauji was a strong proponent of focus. From my early childhood, he would insist that I focus on what I needed to achieve. "All of your senses need to be focused on one project at a time," he would say. "Once you have completed the project to your satisfaction, only then you can move to the next project." This insight and advice were extremely helpful for me after I was selected to be one of the students at the National Dairy Research Institute (NDRI).

I experienced growth and development at the NDRI as never before, but as I described previously, it was a tough place to be. Our principal, Dr. Dastur, was a strict disciplinarian, but I persevered. Besides coping with the difficult course work and long hours working to take care of the animals, I had another thing to worry about: to win the only available scholarship that would support my education. My family's total income was approximately the same as my college expenses. Unless I earned the merit-based scholarship, I would be going back home. But I was competing with some of the most intelligent and hard-working students, and only a group of 45 were selected from 6,000 applicants for the freshmen batch.

The voice of Bauji continued to echo in my mind, *"Focus on what you want to achieve."* Determined to succeed in completing my education without causing financial hardship for my family, I swore that I would not sleep in my bed unless I won the top merit scholarship. I studied sitting on my wooden chair; I would fall asleep in the same chair, and then I would wake up in the middle of the night and start studying again. I only slept four or five hours a night. With hard work, focus, and luck, I won the scholarship during the very first year, allowing me to pay back my family for all they had spent to send me to school. There was a catch, though. The scholarship had to be won on a merit basis each of the four years of college, meaning that I had to continuously get the highest grades in my class to keep attending. Fortunately, thanks to Bauji for instilling in me the importance of focus, I was able to win the scholarship every year.

## The Foundation of Responsible Financial Management

As I have previously mentioned, Bauji instilled the discipline of saving money in all his children. This habit became second nature for me. I learned to save a portion of whatever I earned. Over my lifetime, the magic of compounding has helped create financial security and well-being for my family. In 1972, when I started working for the Quaker Oats Company, my salary started at $1300 per month. After deductions, my take-home income was about $800 a month. I saved half of that every month until Janet and I got married in 1973. Our savings paid for our wedding, honeymoon, and Janet's move from Columbus, Ohio, to the Chicago area where I lived. Soon after joining me, Janet started a teaching job, and we saved enough money to buy a new home. The habit of saving instilled by Bauji from my early childhood has helped our family to achieve our goals of having enough money to not have to worry about finances and to be able to help others in need.

I believe the principle that nothing great was ever built on a weak foundation is applicable to all of us in two ways. First, in our own lives, it's important to acknowledge that it is never too late to put down a strong foundation. Certainly, you have more to overcome if your foundation was not strong in childhood, but, just as with buildings, you can shore up your foundation after the fact. I recall a story a friend told me about renovations he was doing on his house which uncovered that his back deck was built in a shoddy way. The contractors he hired to do the renovations reinstalled the posts holding up the deck, and that deck has stood strong now for more than a decade. Similarly, we as individuals can put up new "posts." It is never too late to develop healthier habits, to push yourself to strive harder in your personal and professional life, and to reinforce the "cracks" in your foundation. Yes, this is harder to do as you get older, but it is *always* doable.

Second, and perhaps more importantly, it's critical to make a commitment to help future generations have a great foundation right from the start. Maybe you have young children or are contemplating starting a family. There is no better time than now to make sure that you give them everything they need to live lives of contribution, good values, and the desire to strive for excellence.

## Exercise 5: Build a strong foundation for your children

All good men and women leave a legacy for their children that helps those children achieve more than they could otherwise. This could be a financial legacy that allows the next generation to be financially worry free; it could be an intellectual legacy that enables the children to succeed in their chosen pursuits; or it could be a moral legacy of values and principles. By practicing and teaching responsible financial management, by reinforcing the value of education, and by exemplifying good moral character, my father covered all of the above. The major enduring legacy we leave for our future generations is our moral values and principles—the pillars on which the lives of our children are built. So, start early with your children to build good habits and to share your love, your time, your knowledge, and your values and principles. Children learn best by watching the behaviors of their parents. Your effectiveness in getting your children to live your legacy starts with you being the example of your values.

Here is a guide to start:

- Have a clear vision of the kind of people you want your children to be when they grow up. This includes a broad sense of the profession you envision.
- Share and live the values as well as the principles you would like your children to practice.
- Talk to your children about their grandparents and extended family and what you learned from them. Have your children spend time with members of the family who exemplify your desired values.
- Build celebrations around your family customs and encourage your children to participate.
- Discuss your beliefs about social issues, moral guidelines, and religion at the dinner table.

• Spend time asking your children what they accomplished and learned every day.

• Model and teach responsible financial management skills.

• Build self-confidence by acknowledging accomplishments. Reinforce positive behaviors; use negative behaviors as teaching moments.

• Provide empowering feedback. Tell your children what inspires you about them and encourage them to achieve greater heights.

• Encourage your children to keep a daily journal. This journal may include: (1) "What I accomplished today"; (2) "What I learned today"; and (3) "New people I met today".

# Principle #6:
## Whatever You Want to Achieve, Give It Your All

Let's go back to my brother Om for this one. Since he's twelve years older than me, we didn't spend much time together in our parents' household. Recently, though, we've had the opportunity to reflect back on how we were raised and what this meant to each of our lives. A story Om told me during one of these conversations is particularly instructive.

Eighth grade was a crucial year in his education. During that year, he and all the other students in the district would be taking a test to compete for a scholarship. His school was three miles away which, in pre-Partition India was a much more time-consuming distance than it might seem now. Om would either walk to school or take his bike, traveling slowly on dirt roads the entire way. Often, by the time he got to school, he was already exhausted.

"'Bauji felt that I would be better off if I stayed close to the school and spent that time studying for the competitive test," Om told me. "So, a decision was made that I would move to a boarding house that was near the school. Nobody asked me if I wanted to go to the boarding house. They just took me there unceremoniously. A cot, a small table, and a wooden chair with no cushion were waiting for me in a large room. The room had many other cots, a few open closets, and a rough jute tarp on the floor. I soon learned that this would be the place for eighteen students for the next three months."

I asked him how it felt to be away from home.

"It was awful at first. But in a couple of days, I got so focused on my studies that I forgot about everything else. Six students out of the eighteen would be selected to be on the team to go for the competitive test to win one available scholarship. All of us wanted to be selected for the team to have a chance at winning that scholarship. For three months we studied hard. At night, Bauji and the other teachers would tutor us and test us on every subject. There was no electricity, so we studied in the dim light of a kerosene lamp. There were no games to play, no other form of entertainment. All we did was study. Once in a while, one of the kids would say something funny or do something mischievous. Bauji would swiftly bring everybody back to their study, saying, 'There will be time for fun after the test.' Everybody would quietly get back to their books.

"None of us slept the night before the test. Fortunately, I was one of the six chosen to take it. All six of us took cold showers early in the morning and got dressed in our bright new white shirts and pajamas. Bauji and the students got into a tonga (a horse-driven cart) for the journey to the test site in Lahore, a city about twelve miles away from our school. As we boarded the tonga, I saw a man with two monkeys, which was considered to be a bad omen. Then, as the tonga moved, the inkpot I was carrying spilled blue ink on my white outfit.

"Even though the day got off to a rocky start, the exam went well for me. When we came out of the test, Bauji grilled each one of us to check how we answered all of the questions, comparing those with the right answers. He was satisfied with my answers. However, he was concerned that I had come out of the test hall fifteen minutes early.

"'Why did you hurry the test?' Bauji said. 'You should have taken your time in writing legibly and reviewing your answers. You know, your handwriting is not the best when you hurry. All your answers are correct, but you may lose some points because of your handwriting and lose the chance of winning the scholarship. You need to learn to pay attention to details. It is not enough to have the right answers; it is important to have a good presentation as well.'

"Five weeks passed. At the young age of twelve, when most kids were playing, I was still sweating over the details of the test and wondering if I was going to get the scholarship. One evening, Bauji came home with a letter from the District Board of Education.

"'Om, my son, you have done it—you won the scholarship! You are the only one.' He picked me up and gave me a kiss on my forehead.

"I felt as if I was on top of the clouds—flying high, feeling great. It had been a tough four months, but it was all worth it. It was one of the defining moments of my life. I learned the importance of hard work, I learned the importance of single-minded focus on whatever you want to achieve, and I learned the feeling of joy that comes with the results of this focus and hard work. This would become my modus operandi for the rest of my life and the basis for whatever I have been able to achieve."

What Om was talking about was the reward gained from approaching any pursuit with total dedication. As you know, Bauji was particularly passionate about education, but he would have implored Om to try as hard as he could to succeed at whatever enterprise he undertook. This is because Bauji understood that if something was worth doing, it was worth doing with all of your heart. How many of us can truly succeed at something we approach casually? It might be fine to be less than committed to a hobby or something you are doing to pass the time. But when it comes to the things that are fundamental to who you are and who you want to be, nothing less than absolute dedication is acceptable. Om didn't want to live away from home for three months at the age of twelve. He didn't want to study all day and all night. But even at that age, he had learned from Bauji that this was the only way he was going to be able to achieve such a difficult goal. That insight helped Om achieve professional and financial success and helped the generations that have followed make outstanding accomplishments. Each of Om's children have built happy, successful families, and most of them have excelled in their professional fields of pursuits. Talk to any accomplished person and you will hear similar stories of absolute dedication. In 1983, I had an opportunity to meet the well-known management guru, Peter Drucker, and he reinforced this point for me. His number one piece of advice: "Stay monomaniacally focused on whatever you really want to accomplish."

## Exercise 6: Plan for success

- In a journal, write down a project that you *really* want to complete.
- Write down what you need to do to accomplish your desired goal.
- Write down your plan, milestones, and measures of success.
- If the project has multiple components, break it down to short and medium-term sub-goals.
- Start working on your plan and stay focused.

- Measure and record your progress.
- Persevere until you achieve the desired goal.
- Repeat the process with another project.

# Principle #7:
## Set High Goals and Work Hard to Achieve Them

My brother Om shared another experience with me about an important lesson he learned from Bauji when he was in the second grade in Pakistan.

"One day, Bauji left to do some chores. Before leaving, he gave me math work to be completed before his return. From the front courtyard through the open front door, I could see the village children playing *Guli Danda* (a favorite Indian game). I wanted to play with the children outside, but I knew I had to complete the studies that my father wanted me to finish before his return. Tears flowing down my cheeks, I would continue to study and solve the math problems Bauji expected me to finish that day.

"The habit of hard work was imbedded so deeply in my mind that it became an essential part of my life. This is evident from the fact that I educated myself without any regular school or guidance while working full time to achieve the level of Master of Arts as a private student. During this time, I also had a job in the Indian Railways department.

Jobs in India were difficult to get with hundreds of applicants vying for a single job."

Here he laughed with a tinge of sarcasm.

"The job was that of an assistant clerk. It was a government job. Anybody with half a brain could do that job in a couple of hours per day. I learned that I could do the job in about an hour a day. I could have lived the comfortable life of a government employee, but I recalled Bauji's words: 'Set high goals for yourself and do not accept mediocrity.' I used the time that remained during the workday to study and take tests that would lead to advancement and promotion within the Railway department. I advanced in my professional career to the position of audit officer in the Indian Drug and Pharmaceutical Limited organization, followed by a position as cost controller in Jaipur Metal and Electrical Company, and eventually became a general manager of the well-known global company, Singer."

What Om learned from Bauji benefited his entire family, as he has passed this teaching along to them. Om's son, Rajeev has grown up to be a bright and accomplished technology and business executive and has a great future ahead of him. He has two daughters, Asha and Meera, both in college as I write this, and both of whom are doing well.

Om's oldest daughter, Jyoti, has prospered with her husband Anil, and raised two sons, Tarun and Kunal. Both have done well in their education and are prospering in their careers. One is a doctor and the other is an engineer—just what Bauji would have wished. The generational legacy continues.

Om's younger daughter, Neetu, is a bright, strong-willed, and caring young lady. Neetu is a consummate professional, working as an editor, helping her husband, Vinay, with his business, and taking good care of her family.

All this accomplishment started from the same place: setting your sights high and then working diligently to reach those goals. Those two things work in concert. Too often, people shy away from ambitious goals, believing that they need to be "realistic" about their options when, in fact, this realism is nothing more than setting an unnecessary limitation on your life. At the same time, there are many who have big dreams but don't have the willingness to do everything required to achieve those dreams. I'm sure you know several people who talk big about what they are going to do with their lives, but aren't willing to make the necessary sacrifices to get there. How many of those people ever come anywhere close to their dreams? What Bauji understood, even before there was a clear path to achieving one's ambitions in India, was that it is *both* high goals and extremely hard work that get you where you want to go.

It is also clear to me now that the benefits of a strong foundation of values and principles last for generations. As I have previously shared, I have led research and development departments at multiple

Fortune 100 companies. In each case, my teams developed a portfolio of growth projects. This portfolio normally consisted of short-term, medium-term, and long-term projects. The short-term projects (called the Horizon I projects) consisted of tasks that could be completed in less than 18 months; the medium-term projects (called the Horizon II projects) would last up to three years, and the long-term projects (called the Horizon III projects) generally were those that would take more than three years to complete. The objective of all these projects was to provide business growth. The intent was that Horizon I projects would take minimal resources and provide incremental growth (or prevent downward trends) with very low risk. The Horizon II projects would take more resources and provide higher growth opportunities than those in Horizon I. The highest-risk and highest-potential-reward projects were in Horizon III, and these required much more investment.

There was one additional level, though very few projects fell in this area. This level is what I call generational growth, and these are projects geared toward transforming the company. One embarks on a generational growth project if the very existence of the company is in question. That seemed to be the case when I joined the Pepsi Cola Beverage Company, a division of PepsiCo.

The year was 1984. The President of the US division of Pepsi Cola was 38-year old Roger Enrico. He invited his top leadership team to formulate a go-forward strategy for Pepsi Cola, and he started with the following comments:

> I have asked many business analysts about the future of Pepsi Cola. They tell me that the cola business in the US is a mature category. Our prospects of growth are dim. Cola consumption is almost half of the total liquid consumption in the US. The heaviest consumers of cola beverages are teenagers, and the population trend of the US is not in our favor. On top of that, Coke is a formidable competitor, winning the majority share of business away from us. We need a strategy to transform our business to ensure that we are around for many generations to come. With this team, I believe we have the best chance to come up with that strategy and a plan.

I had just joined the company. All of us knew the history of Pepsi. Pepsi had gone bankrupt a couple of times; first in 1923 and again in 1931. It even tried to sell itself to Coke during the Great Depression. The team led by Enrico was not going to let Pepsi Cola repeat history. In my professional career, this was the first time a team had focused on ensuring a legacy of generational growth. The foundation built by Enrico and his team secured the future of Pepsi-Co as is evident now.

A plan for generational growth is just as important and applicable to personal life as it is to professional life. One time, when I was reviewing my Horizon I, II, and III project portfolios with one of my advisers, he off-handedly commented, "This is well thought out to provide growth opportunities for the next ten to fifteen years. Have you ever thought about what your 250-year project is?" The question hit me like a ton of bricks. I do not know if Bauji thought in those exact terms but transforming the future of coming generations has been the outcome of Bauji's actions.

I am troubled when I hear people say that most people in the US are living from paycheck to paycheck and can't think about the future or that young people are too focused on instant gratification to think about the future. The words of Bauji still echo in my mind: "My obligation as well as privilege is to leave my children better off than I am; I expect my children to do the same for their children." If you have children, or plan to have children, I urge you to start developing a strategy and a plan to improve the lives of your future generations. That could be the project that continues your legacy for 100, 200, or even 250 years.

## Exercise 7: Your 250-year project

This exercise will have a generational impact on your family if you have children or plan to have children. So, spend considerable time thinking about this and executing it:

- What is your ONE Horizon IV (Generational Growth) project that will have a lasting impact on your children and your grandchildren?
- Develop a strategy and a plan for success with this project.
- Allocate 15-20 percent of your time every day to this project.

# Principle #8:
# Education Is the Only Way
# Out of Poverty

When I was eight years old, our family was living in the little village of Pandori with adobe houses, dirt streets, no electricity, and no running water. I was playing in the street with a couple of my friends when I saw a beggar approach our home. My mother opened the old wooden door of our courtyard and asked the beggar to wait outside while she went in to get him some food. When she returned, I ran toward my mother and wrapped myself around her legs.

"Is that your son?" the beggar asked her.

"Yes," she said as she ran her fingers through my dirty hair.

"Enjoy him while you can; he won't be with you too long."

My mother was shocked to hear this, and she reacted as though she had been threatened. "Why did you say that?"

The beggar obviously understood how my mother had interpreted his statement, and he spoke quickly to clarify. "No, no, I don't mean that any harm will come to him. I mean, he will not live with you for long. He will leave you and India for some foreign country. He will marry somebody there and live in another land."

With those words, the beggar turned and left, leaving my mother dumbfounded. That evening at dinner, my mother told my father about this conversation.

"How is it even possible?" she said. "None of us know anything about any country except India."

My father looked up from his *thali* (plate of food). "Anything is possible. Our job is to prepare our children by building a good foundation. The life they build on that foundation is up to them."

My father always believed that a huge part of that foundation was education, and he lived this every day. As the headmaster of the adobe school nearby, he was a strong disciplinarian and we studied hard even though the condition of the school was primitive. Kids sat on a tarp strip on the dirt floor in a straight line with the teacher in front of them. Any mischief was punished with a stick to the rear or the palm of the hand. This discipline paid off when Bauji took five kids to a state scholarship contest after completion of the fourth grade and won five scholarships out of the six allocated to the entire school district.

When I finished fourth grade myself, I had come to the end of my potential schooling in Pandori. While nearly all my classmates ended their education at that point, my parents agreed to send me to Khemkaran, about forty miles away, to live with my uncle and continue to go to school. While

forty miles might not sound like much now, transportation in India was so poor at the time that the
trip took nearly an entire day. We had to walk about
two-and-a-half miles to get to the train station, and
the train trip itself was more than three hours, as-
suming everything ran on schedule, which was the
case only half the time. It was also expensive, with
each trip costing a significant percentage of Bauji's
monthly income.

When I finished fifth grade, I begged my parents
to let me come back to live with them in Pandori. My
brother Dwarka would be going to a high school about
five miles away in a village called Varpal; Bauji gave
me the option of going back to school in Khemkaran
or walking that distance with my brother every day to
go to school in Varpal. It didn't take me any time to
decide: I would much rather walk five miles each way
than be away from my parents and my brother again.

These were tough years. Dwarka and I would
wake up very early in the morning, do our chores,
and then walk through the muddy fields to get to
the school. After attending classes, we would walk
back and then do our homework and more chores.
After two years, Dwarka went to a school in a larger
city, Amritsar, to finish his Faculty of Science degree (twelfth grade). I moved along with him.

Throughout all of this, Bauji made sure that I
did well in school, asking me about every single test
I took. He wanted me to be the best. He would ask
if I stood first in my class in every subject. For the

longest time, I could only claim to be outperforming my fellow students in seven out of eight. Finally, though, I could claim to be the top student in every class. I recall how excited I was. I wanted to tell Bauji so badly, but I had to wait until the next morning while we fetched the feed for the buffalo.

"So, how did you do in the tests?" he asked.

With my chest expanded with pride, I told him that I stood first in every subject.

We continued walking, and a few minutes later, he asked me what each of my grades were. I told him that I got 96 out of 100 in English, 92 in Geography, 98 in Math . . .

Suddenly he stopped in his tracks. "How could you lose two points in Math?" he said.

As my chest deflated, I told him I did not know. Later, I checked and determined that I had made a minor mistake that cost me those two points.

When I reported this to him, he said, "I want you to always do your best. And when you make a mistake, I want you to learn from it." This was a lesson I would never forget.

For my high school education, I stayed in Amritsar and went to DAV High School. I lived with my brother Om in a place known as The Quarter. It was a row of little apartments on a main road right next to a train track. We had a small dirt floor space of about 12' x 10' that served as the sleeping area during the summer when it was too hot to sleep in the room. Beyond that space was an open sewer, and once you crossed the sewer, there was a road with streetlights. Many Indian kids studied under the streetlights at night. I did this as well for a while during the summer when the temperatures inside the concrete building got unbearably hot. Eventually, I worked out a way of extending the electrical cable from inside The Quarter to the outside wall where I hung a light bulb. There was not much to do for entertainment. All I did was go to school, study, eat my meals, and study some more. This helped me prepare for doing well in competitive exams for potential entry into a good college.

DAV High School was highly competitive and had a lot more students than I was used to. I felt lost, alone, and insignificant. Fortuitously, a great blessing in my life came in the form of good friends. I met my best friend Mohinder Chanana. He was pretty serious about excelling in education. He was also brilliant, which provided me an incentive to compete. He came from a similar background to mine, and his father was a policeman who stressed the same values Bauji stressed. His mother was an exceptionally kind woman who practically adopted me as her son. Mohinder and I would study together in Company Bagh, a nice park in Amritsar. His home was close to these gardens, and most of the time he would drag me to his house for lunch or dinner.

Both Mohinder and I were driven to excel in the final high school exams which, as I have previously described, determined the fate of all graduates. The students with top grades got a choice to attend the most prestigious colleges or universities while others would have to forego college education. In order to take these finals, every student had to pay an entrance fee. A significant percentage of the students could not afford the entrance fee and would drop out of high school. One such student happened to be a friend of mine, Vishwa. He was ready to drop out. I had saved some money from the allowance my brother Om gave me every month, but it would not cover the total fee. So, I approached Mohinder. All our families were of modest means and had very little to spare. Regardless, Mohinder asked his father to cover the entrance fee for Vishwa. Mohinder's father took all the money he had saved and gave it to Mohinder to ensure that Vishwa would be able to pay the fees for his finals. This act of kindness happened in 1959, over sixty years ago but it is as fresh in my mind as if it happened yesterday. From that day on, Mohinder became my model of kindness and great friendship.

My school years were an endless challenge but, because of Bauji, I never lost sight of the ultimate goal. Having grown up poor and being surrounded by other poor people, I knew that the only way out of poverty for me would be through education. This is as true today all over the world as it was then for me in India. Today, as I sit in my home in Flower Mound, Texas, I cannot help but marvel at the prediction of that beggar and the empowering belief of my father. When I recently reminded my sister, Pushpa, of the beggar's prediction, she shook her head, saying, "Never in a million years could we have imagined in Pandori that this would be your life." But it is a life I never would have had if my father hadn't been so persistent that I get the best possible education.

While you might think that the opportunity to get a great education has passed you by, I'm convinced that this is not the case and that education can always make a positive difference in your life. Whether it means going to night classes at a community college, taking online courses, enrolling in a technical school, or even reading every book and watching every instructional video you can get your hands on, there are chances for you to learn more and use what you've learned to improve your station in life.

And if there are children in your life, I implore you to treat education with them the way Bauji used it with me. Make it a priority and instill in them a passion for learning and a desire to apply what they learn to make a difference in their futures. I know it made things happen for me, and I know with certainty that my situation was not in any way anomalous.

## Exercise 8: Leverage observations and insights for continuous improvement

We learn through formal education as well as through observations and experiences. We can also supplement our education by learning from other people's experiences. Integrating those learnings into insights and acting on those insights can be enormously helpful in your growth. Toward that end, I'd like you to keep a daily journal. In it, be sure to include:

- What did you learn today from your and other's experiences? What insights have you developed from what you learned?
- How can you use what you learned to improve the lives of your family members and future generations?
- What are the specific actions you plan to take?

# Principle #9:
## You Must Make the Tough Choices to Be Successful in Life

Earlier I mentioned Dr. Gurcharan Singh Randhawa who is a highly successful retired medical doctor in Marshalltown, Iowa. He was born in my little village of Pandori when Bauji was the school headmaster. He would be the first one to tell you that never in his life in Pandori could he have imagined that he would ultimately find himself practicing medicine in the United States.

The first time I met Gurcharan, he was a little kid. I think it was 1952, and he was four years old, four years younger than me. His parents lived on the same street as we did. I was just leaving my school in Pandori when he started first grade with Bauji as his teacher. Gurcharan referred to my father as *Master ji* (respected teacher). His parents were very helpful to the people in the village and became good friends with my mother and father.

When I left for the United States in 1966, I lost contact with most of the people in Pandori. So, it was a surprise when, in 1976, I got a call from Gurcharan in Buffalo Grove, Illinois, a suburb of Chicago. He was now twenty-seven, doing his internship in pharmacology, and working as a pharmacist.

We met and talked about how our lives had evolved over the years. Gurcharan had accomplished much in the ensuing time, but he never forgot the foundation my father provided him.

"I could not have done this without the valuable guidance of *Master ji*," he said softly, his eyes moistening. "He has been the guiding light for my life."

Gurcharan cleared his throat and continued. "Besides teaching me the value of education, *Master ji* drilled in me the importance of making difficult choices to achieve what I wanted out of life. I had seen my parents struggle to make ends meet in that little village. I was determined to create a better life for myself, for my parents, my siblings, and my future family. *Master ji* advised me that besides working hard, I would have to make some very tough choices, including leaving Pandori to pursue higher education and selecting the right subjects to study for a successful career. With his advice, I chose science and math during my high school and early college education and that helped me get into the College of Pharmacy. I finished my MS in pharmacology in India and then made the tough choice of leaving India and my family to come to the US."

Gurcharan and I stayed in touch for a while and then fell out of contact again as so often happens when people are in the midst of building their lives. We would not see each other for a couple of decades, but we reconnected after this long stretch through, of all things, mutual acquaintances in Pandori. By this point, Gurcharan was no longer a pharmacist, as he had become an MD. I asked him what led to this transition.

"After my internship at the Rush Hospital in Chicago, I continued to work as a pharmacist for many years. I got a job as Assistant Director of Pharmacy at the Provident Hospital in Chicago. One day, I got a prescription slip from a doctor. The medicine was new, and I felt that the doctor had made a mistake in prescribing the dosage level. I called the doctor to check if I was reading the slip correctly. The doctor got quite defensive and thought I was challenging him.

"'I am the doctor,' he said, 'and you are the pharmacist. Your job is to fill the prescription.'

"'I can't possibly fill a prescription that may harm a patient,' I told the doctor. 'I am just asking you to check the dosage level since this is a new medicine.' The doctor got really upset and reported me to the hospital. Irrespective of the fact that the Pharmacy and Therapeutics committee reviewed the case in my favor, the doctor sent nasty letters to my hospital saying that I had insulted him. I will have to admit, I felt that the doctor was looking down not only on my profession but also insulting my heritage because I am a turban-bearing Sikh from India. That day, I determined to become a doctor.

"I took my MCAT exams and entered medical school against all odds. I was not a citizen of the US yet. I had just been blessed with a daughter, Jyoti. She was three months old when I started medical school, and, by the time I became a full-fledged doctor, she had turned eight years old. All during medical school I supported myself by working as a pharmacist at night."

Gurcharan was faced with another difficult choice after that encounter with the doctor. He knew that getting his MD was going to be extremely hard work at a time when he already had a good job and he had enormous family responsibilities. The easier decision would have been to continue to do what he had been doing, but what the doctor had shown him was that there was a yawning need for people who would take the profession as seriously as possible. And, just as important, it was a role that Gurcharan was committed to fill. So, he made the difficult choice, sacrificed a portion of his family life, and came out the other side making a much bigger contribution to the world than he ever could have made as a pharmacist. Over the years, he has helped more than a hundred and fifty Indian immigrants establish their lives and their businesses in the United States while also helping to bring electricity and good drinking water to the village in which he was born. He never would have been able to do that without the resources that being a doctor provided him.

"Everything I wanted to achieve, including improving the lives of my parents, my siblings, and my family, happened due to the tough choices I have made in my life. I am so happy that I have been able to make a difference in the lives of many of my family members, my friends, and the people of Pandori."

Having spent the first 21 years of my life in India and the last 54 years in the United States, I understand the cultural differences in the two countries. When I was growing up in India, there were not many choices to be made. Financially strapped parents, who were culturally immersed in making sure that their children had a better life, chose allocating most of their money on education as the top priority. The choices in consumer products were limited to only a few selections. In the US, the choices in everything are almost limitless and paralyzing. My wife, Janet, tells a story of her friend Shirley going to the grocery store to buy a breakfast cereal for her husband. She walked through the aisle full of cereal boxes making all kinds of claims about the amount of sugar and the different levels of fiber they contained, whether they included pre- or probiotics, were made from whole grains, were gluten free, and many other distinctions. Shirley was so confused and stressed that she walked out of the store without buying any cereal at all.

The fast food restaurant McDonald's was one of the first to recognize that consumers found an abundance of choices difficult and confusing. They simplified a package of choices for the customers as a Meal #1, #2, #3 &c. where the individual products were bundled together. This initiative helped speed the ordering process and increased McDonald's' sales.

The process of making difficult choices is further complicated by the constant barrage of commercials on TV, electronic media, and social media suggesting that you do not have to make any choices; you can have it all—and, as a matter of fact, you deserve to have it all. This mindset explains one of the factors that differentiates the financial success of those who immigrate to the US from economically challenged countries such as India and China. The immigrants are better equipped to make tough choices to save money for creating a long-term future for themselves and for their families.

Most of us have or will come face-to-face with moments when our path to true success and satisfaction requires making a very difficult choice. Bauji always believed that making such choices defined us and led us toward our destiny. The challenge, of course, is to weigh how much you desire the life you could have by making the difficult choice against the sacrifices you'll need to make in order to achieve it. In Gurcharan's case, the choice to become a doctor was a defining moment in his life, and he has never regretted making it. Is your defining moment waiting for you? What is the price you're going to have to pay for it?

Not everyone is cut out for making the decisions that Gurcharan made. But Bauji would have been the first to tell you that, when you want to achieve big dreams in your life, you need to be prepared to make some very difficult choices on the path to your desired destination.

## Exercise 9: Test your aptitude for making tough choices

We have multiple resources at our disposal: Financial and other material resources; non-material resources such as time and energy; and intangible resources such as our passion, and emotional capabilities including self-control, stress management, and forgiveness. All these resources are finite, hence the need to make tough choices before we run out of some critical resource that would help us achieve our dreams. Let us choose an easily measurable resource, money, to test your ability to make tough choices. Here is a hypothetical situation:

You are an average wage earner, married with two young children. You are concerned that you have not been able to save much for a rainy day or for your children's education. Imagine that the company you work for has outperformed its targets for sales and profits and has decided to give a one-time bonus to all employees. You have received a bonus of $10,000 that you did not expect.

You have the following options for using the bonus money:

- OPTION #1: You choose to save the after-tax money and put it in a savings account, an investment account, or a 529 plan for your children's education.
- OPTION # 2: You choose to use half of the after-tax money to pay off your credit card bills and put the remaining in savings, an investment account, or a 529 plan.
- OPTION # 3: You choose to celebrate by taking the family out to a nice dinner, allocate half of the remaining after-tax bonus for option #1 or option #2, and plan a modest family vacation with the remaining funds.
- OPTION # 4: You tell yourself that you and your family really deserve to go on a cruise; after all you have not had a good vacation this year. You book a cruise for you and your family, hoping to cover the cost with the after-tax money.

If you chose Option #1 or Option #2, you have a high aptitude for making tough choices.

If you chose Option #3, you have a moderate aptitude for making tough choices.

If you chose Option #4, you value instant gratification over long-term benefits, and you have a low aptitude for making tough choices.

# Principle #10:
# Live Your Life by Your Own Design, Principles, and Values

I was almost fifteen years old when I completed high school. To continue my education, I would now be going to a city called Karnal, which was about 160 miles away from home. It was an emotional time for both my mother and my father. Mom quietly shed her tears, while Bauji wanted to make sure that I had one more discussion with him before I left for college. This was his chance to provide me with parting advice that would help me as I started my life journey almost entirely on my own.

He motioned me to walk with him to one corner of the room and asked my mother to leave us alone for a few minutes. As my mother disappeared outside, he cleared his throat. "Your feet almost fit my shoes," he said. "You are a bright kid and you have just as much or more formal education as I have had. You will be making some important life decisions on your own. You have the smarts and the education, but that does not add up to the wisdom that comes from life experience. Going forward, I can only offer you the advice that is based on wisdom collected over my life. The choice of whether or not you want my advice or whether or not you want to follow my advice is yours. If you run into a situation where you need my advice, you will have to ask. I will be here to offer it to you, but I will not do this without your asking. You can then decide if the advice is helpful."

Even at fifteen, I was awestruck by the wisdom of the man sitting in front of me. I recall having a lump in my throat that prevented me from speaking at all. I wanted to say thank you, but the words just would not come out.

After a few minutes, I gathered my wits, looked at my father, and asked him how he decided to become a teacher. He shifted in his seat, looked out toward the distance—almost as though he were seeking the past—and then started to talk.

"Almost six months had passed since we had left our home in Pakistan. Winter had set in. It was cold and damp most days. Our money had run out, and everybody in the family seemed to be down. All the men were feeling that they were failing in their responsibility of providing for the family. So, your three uncles—Diwan, Girdhari, and Bishambher—and I started looking for either some business opportunities or some work that we could do to earn a living and provide for our families. In Pakistan, Girdhari had a brokerage business between farmers in the area and the shopkeepers who sold fruits, vegetables, grains, and cotton. Girdhari would bring farmers and shopkeepers together in a *mandi* (open market), where the business transactions took place. Girdhari took a commission for his services from both the farmers and the customers. It was quite a lucrative business in Pakistan.

"When things got tough in India after the Partition, Girdhari proposed that all four brothers join up to start the same business in Khemkaran. As you know, the town is fairly small and close to the Pakistan border. Farmers in the area grew wheat, cotton, vegetables, and fruit but had no outlet for their products. The plan was that the brothers would become brokers. The business did not require much investment and, at the very least, would provide food for the family. The oldest brother, Diwan, immediately agreed to join Girdhari. Bishambher offered to work on a part-time basis but wanted to start his own separate fabric business. I had to decide whether to join my brothers or to do something that was more in line with my talents and values. I needed to give this some serious thought. I considered what I wanted for the future of our family. Yes, I wanted to earn enough money to put food on the table, but I also wanted to make sure that I could prepare my children for a better future and to be able to help other people. I had been a teacher in Pakistan. I liked teaching, and I felt as though I was helping to improve the community. I believed that I could achieve my desired outcomes by teaching, although the salary of a teacher was barely enough for survival. If I joined my brothers in their business quest, I could make more money, but I would not be able to live my values of educating my children and others to prepare them for a brighter future. Also, with the state of literacy in India at the time, I believed that I could help a lot more children by going into teaching. I felt that teaching was my calling. Fortunately, there was a shortage of teachers in India at the time, because the government had made education a top priority post-independence and this had led them to create many jobs in the field. After spending a few sleepless nights, I decided that going into business with my brothers, as lucrative as it might be, was not in line with my values. I applied for a teaching job and I have been teaching ever since. My brothers have made a lot more money than I have, but I am still happy with the decision I made."

I had been intently listening to Bauji without looking at him directly. As he paused, I glanced up at his face and realized that his expression matched his words; he seemed to be at peace.

"It is not enough to simply focus on what outcomes you want to achieve; it is also important to follow your values when you decide how to go about getting to your goals," I said to confirm that I understood his message.

Bauji nodded his head in approval. "Yes, you need to know what you want to achieve and decide how you want to go about achieving it. For example, if your desired goal is to be rich, you could earn the right to be rich by working hard or by robbing a bank. The *how* is just as important as the *what* in achieving your goal."

As you have come to see by now, Bauji focused strongly on making sure we were as prepared as possible to achieve success. But an equally strong message—and one that I believe is fundamental to the way we should all live our lives—is that our success should be in concert with our values. I have known many people who have achieved financial success or acclaim within their fields who feel empty inside because that success has come at the cost of their values. And I have known many other people who might not have as much money or might not be as esteemed in their fields but who have a deep sense of contentment because they have achieved what they achieved without compromising their key values. At times, there are tough choices to be made. In the early stages of parenthood, I made some tough choices to ensure financial well-being of the family at the expense of spending enough quality time with them. I am happy to see that our son Daven has developed a better work-life balance to spend time with his wife and children.

For the sake of ourselves as individuals and for the sake of our society, I think it is important for everyone to pursue the greatest success that aligns most closely with their values. There is no question that my father could have made more money going into business with his brothers. Our family would have lived a more comfortable life, and we would have had fewer financial struggles. But doing that would have made him less than he wanted to be—and the world would be lesser for it. When I think about the number of lives Bauji affected in a positive way and how those people have gone on to contribute to their communities and the world, I can't help but believe that we would all be poorer if my father had compromised his values to enrich himself. I implore you to develop a work-life balance that is in line with your desired family and career goals.

# Exercise 10: Create your future by your own design

- What type of work or career are you really passionate about?
- Is your current career pursuit aligned with your passion and your values?
- If yes, what steps would you take to accelerate your progress?
- If not, what is your plan for change…
    o  5 year plan
    o  1·year plan
    o  100 day plan
- What would you do differently tomorrow?

# Principle #11:
# Focus on What is Really Important to Achieve Your Goals

Only a few people had much of an education in Pandori when I was growing up and this had a significant effect on health, quality of life, and the life expectancy of the population. The village had no doctors or medical facilities. There was limited knowledge of sanitation or nutrition. Death during the birthing process—either the death of the baby or the death of the mother—was quite common. My parents themselves lost two children, one of whom was stillborn and the other who died at birth.

I was almost a casualty as well.

Pandori was our sanctuary, and for a while it seemed it would be the last place I would ever see. Conditions in the village were generally unsanitary, and it turned out that I was an excellent host to pathogenic germs and parasites. At the age of five, I developed amoebic dysentery, apparently from drinking unsafe water. With no doctor in the village, my mother would carry me for miles to a village named Gohalwar to catch a bus to the city, where she would implore every doctor she could find to give me a miracle medicine to rid me of this disease. There were only a few doctors in the city, and most would turn my mother away because they thought she had no money to pay for the treatment. She would plead, she would beg, and she would appeal to their sense of decency and even their sense of shame. I remember one time when she fell to the feet of a doctor and latched on to him, refusing to let go until he agreed to examine me.

Sometimes, a doctor would take pity and see me, but none of them could offer any kind of cure. One doctor even told my mother, "Take him home and let him die peacefully, old lady. No doctor can do anything for him." After that, tears streaming down her cheeks, Bhabiji bundled me in a cotton sheet and walked out into the pouring rain. We walked to the city's horse buggy stand and boarded it for the village for what my mother thought would be my final journey. During the slow ten-mile ride through the wind and the rain, I slipped in and out of consciousness. When I awoke one time, I found my mother holding me very close to her, still crying, looking up at the gray sky and pleading to God to spare me. In a moment of lucidity, I reached toward her, wiped her tears, and said, "Don't worry Bhabiji; I am not going to die."

The next day, Bauji took me to our local medicine man who generally sat in the village square with other influential people. My father had been reluctant to do this, because he believed that medicine men represented a more primitive time before the development of modern medical practice, and he was convinced that we needed to move beyond these times. But the situation had gotten desperate, and Bauji had no intention of giving up without a fight.

When Bauji approached him, the medicine man regarded my father indignantly.

"So, you finally brought him to me," he said, "now that all doctors have given up on him."

Bauji was embarrassed, yet resolute.

"We really need your help. I will be forever grateful."

The medicine man looked around at the other people in the square as if to say, "Let this be a lesson to all of you. I am the man to come to when you are sick." Then, he started gathering some herbs, grinding them with honey using a mortar and pestle until the mixture turned into a thick paste. He gave that paste to Bauji, telling my father that I was to have one spoonful of the treatment every day and that the rest of my diet needed to be strictly limited. For three months, I ate the paste, bland scrambled eggs, rice, yogurt, and moong dal soup. The monotony of it was frustrating for me, but I couldn't argue with the results. Slowly but steadily, the medicine man's prescription allowed me to recover from the invading microbial attack.

Obviously, this story illustrates the depth of my parents' love for me and their commitment to doing whatever it took to return me to health. But it also tells another story, one that had larger ramifications for the village and one that serves as a lesson for all of us. While I was recovering, Bauji made an effort to learn everything he could about the cause of my sickness, reading any relevant book that was available at the time. Once he understood what had attacked my system, it became a priority to him that not only I never face this again but that the entire village be safe from it. He learned to dramatically improve the quality of the drinking water. During the monsoon season, he would advise everyone to boil their water before drinking. He learned to treat the water in the well by using an oxidizing agent, potassium permanganate, to kill the disease-causing bacteria and other microorganisms living in the well. And he had the well covered to prevent organic debris from falling into it. Once this became his mission, he refused to let up until he had made conditions better for everyone.

If you are reading this book, it's likely that you won't face a problem similar to the one Bauji needed to solve here. But his method to solving it is the real message I'm trying to convey. Bauji understood the importance of improving the drinking water in Pandori. This was something that was going to affect generations. And he also understood that he could not go about fixing the problem casually. He needed to educate himself, he needed to develop a plan, and he needed to take action.

What things are most important to you? How focused are you on accomplishing what you need to accomplish? What Bauji taught us was that one cannot pursue essential goals casually. Essential goals must be pursued with total dedication. If this means sacrificing some less important things, so be it. Starting every day with a plan for how you are going to get closer to achieving your biggest goals is critical if you are actually going to achieve them.

## Exercise 11: The wisdom introspection

Bauji had a limited formal education, only completing the eighth grade. However, his wisdom extended far beyond his formal education. He learned by observing, doing research by reading about any problem he faced and talking to other people, integrating his knowledge into insights, and then applying his insights to solving problems faced by his family or the village. Wisdom, I have come to realize, is more than formal education—it is the process of integrating intellect, education, information, observations, and experiences into knowledge; extracting insights from that knowledge; and applying those insights to solving problems or creating new opportunities.

Please answer the following questions on a 1-5 scale with:

> 1: strongly disagree
> 2: somewhat disagree

3: neither agree nor disagree
4: somewhat agree
5: strongly agree

1 – I make it a point to learn new things by observing, reading, listening to others, and through personal experiences.
2 – I enjoy being exposed to new experiences and to diverse viewpoints.
3 – It is important for me to apply my new knowledge to solving problems or creating new opportunities for others.
4 – I can filter and overcome my negative emotions rapidly.
5 – It is important for me to understand and continuously improve my thinking and actions.
6 – I tend to postpone making major decisions as long as I can.

Add up your score for questions 1-5 minus your score for question 6. If your score is above 20, you are in the top 10 percentile in wisdom score. If your score is 10 or less, it is time to find a coach to help you navigate.

# Principle #12:
# Never Forget Where You Came From

"You will do what I told you to do. I will fire your a\*\* if you don't, and you will have nothing and be nothing," yelled my boss as he pointed his finger at me from across his desk. The year was 1976, and I had been working as a scientist in a food company in the US for a couple of years after receiving my PhD from The Ohio State University. I loved my job, and I was good at developing new technologies. My boss seemed to like my work, but from time to time, he would make strange requests. He was yelling at me at the moment over one such request that I found to be unethical. He had asked me to buy an expensive camera for scientific purposes but then he wanted me to put that camera in his car so he could take it home for his personal use. I had a choice to make: steal from the company for my boss, or risk losing my job.

Then I recalled the words of my father: "Never forget where you came from." I was not quite sure what he meant at the time, but experience had given me two key insights from that advice. One was that I should draw strength from the fact that our family had very little when I grew up and we were able to survive and thrive after multiple difficult times. The second was that we should pay forward the help we received during the times we needed it from others.

At this time, the first insight seemed appropriate. Our family had gone through many tough times and had not only survived them but ultimately thrived in the face of them. As you know, we had lost everything during the Partition of India, including our home and all other assets. I myself was actually living what I considered to be a "bonus life" (or maybe more than one) as I previously wrote about my mother rescuing me from potential death when I was left behind by our caravan from Pakistan to India and when I was deathly ill in Pandori.

With this in mind, I asked myself, "Why should I be afraid of losing my job? I should do what I believe is right. I can survive if I lose my job, but can I live with the knowledge that I did something unethical to keep my job?"

With these thoughts swirling in my head, I looked up at my boss and told him that I could not, in good conscience, buy a camera with the company funds for his personal use. To my surprise, he turned his chair, faced me and said, "Glad to know that you would not do that. Now I can be sure that you will give me your honest opinion and not be just another lackey who would do anything I demand."

This incident provided me with a lot of confidence in handling future tough situations. I was faced with a similar tough choice in 1984 when I joined Pepsi Cola Beverage Company, a division of PepsiCo, as Vice President of Research and Development. Pepsi had a hard-charging culture. As a matter of fact, one of the consultants from McKinsey that Pepsi had retained to examine the culture described Pepsi's executive team as "people highly driven by fear to achieve exceptional business growth." Most employees were in constant fear of losing their jobs. Soon after I joined the company, a colleague of mine told me that "a bullet is fired with your name on it as soon as you are hired. You can dodge that bullet for a while, but it is only a matter of time before it catches up with you." With this as a cultural background, it was pretty normal for individual employees to throw their subordinates or colleagues under the bus for mistakes they themselves had made.

Despite this, I was doing pretty well as head of R&D. It was inevitable, though, that either I or my staff would make a mistake someday. That day arrived a few years after I had joined the company. For cost-reduction purposes, we decided to change the sweetener in Pepsi Cola. My team was in charge of managing the development of the new Pepsi. In the process of finalizing the new formula, one of my scientists made a calculation mistake. We launched the new product and then realized that the calculation mistake would cost our franchisees more than a million dollars.

As soon as the scientist realized his mistake, he came to me. He was shaking like a leaf, afraid that he was going to be fired for this. I thanked him for his honesty and told him not to worry. I then went to my boss, Bennett Nussbaum, who had been my strong supporter and mentor. Bennett was deeply concerned by this news. "Enrico is not going to be happy," he said, speaking about our CEO, Roger Enrico. He suggested that we discuss this with our CFO, Fred Miles.

Fred was not very encouraging.

"Nobody has ever walked into Roger's office with a bad piece of news and walked out without being fired," he said.

With this in mind, I made the appointment to see Roger Enrico. Fred came along with me and, as we walked from Fred's office to Enrico's, Fred put his hand on my shoulder. "It was great knowing you Surinder," he said. "We will miss you around here."

As was normally the case at Pepsi, I had a presentation ready to share with Enrico. I took him through the presentation, sharing the background and the complex calculations the scientist had made. The last slide was about our go-forward options. There were three. Option 1 was to admit the mistake and cover the cost for our franchisees. Option 2 was to cover the cost by slashing the R&D budget by a million dollars. Option 3 was to change the formula without telling anybody or admitting the mistake. Roger focused intently on that last slide and then asked me for my recommendation.

"Roger, my recommendation is to tell the franchisees that we made a mistake and cover their costs. It was R&D's mistake, so I am willing to cover the cost by slashing my R&D budget. Although I can change the formulation and nobody will know, our credibility will be at stake if I do not admit that we made a mistake. Our credibility is worth more than a million dollars."

"How much is the total cost, Fred?" asked Enrico.

"It is around a million dollars," replied Fred.

"Well, find a way to cover it from our profit and loss. I do not want to hurt our R&D work."

As we walked out of Enrico's office, Fred had a look of disbelief.

"I have never seen somebody walk out of Enrico's office with his head held high after making such a mistake. What gave you the courage to make that recommendation, and what would you have done if you had gotten fired?"

"Fairly simple Fred," I replied. "It was something that my father said a long time ago: 'Do what you believe is right; don't let the fear of consequences hold you back from acting on your beliefs.' As far as what I would have done if I got fired, I have lived through a lot worse in the past. I can afford to take the risks because I have the confidence that I will find a way to make it through tough times."

Like most people, I have gone through peaks and valleys during my lifetime. During the valleys I have faced as an adult, I have drawn courage and confidence from my recall of where my family came from and how we had always overcome adversity. As bad as any situation might be, the probability of that situation being as bad as the Partition of India is extremely low. And even if a catastrophic event came to pass, I know we will work hard and be stronger for the adversity once again. Every time I recall the events of our family overcoming adversities, I develop a stronger and more empowering belief that we will be the victors and not the victims of tough times.

You might have never faced situations as dire as being torn from your home or facing extreme illness with no available medical help, but you've almost certainly faced times when things seemed at their bleakest. If, when you face adversity, you use the memory of those times to show that you can get to the other side, you will not only survive but thrive.

## Exercise 12: What are your beliefs?

Our beliefs define what we can or cannot do. As Henry Ford once said, "Whether you think you can, or you think you can't—you're right."

- What are your beliefs about what you can achieve in your life?
- What are your beliefs about your capabilities and strengths?

- What are your beliefs about your limitations?
- When things are not going well, what are your beliefs about your ability to bounce back and succeed in life?

Here is an exercise for you to discover your hidden talents and abilities that will help you face future adversities. For one hour, be by and with yourself in a calm and serene environment.

- Recall one of the worst cases of adversity you have faced in your life.
- Recall and write down how low, helpless, and desperate you felt when you faced that adversity.
- Recall how you marshalled your inner resources to overcome that adversity.
- Recall the feeling of triumph and relief after overcoming that adversity.
- Write down your insights and the special talents and abilities that helped you during that time.

- What did you come to believe after coming through that adversity?

Now recall a positive, successful, exhilarating event in your life.

- How did you achieve that success?
- What strengths and capabilities led you to achieve that success?
- What did you learn about yourself?
- What are your beliefs about yourself after that success?

# Principle #13:
## Wherever You Go, Leave the Place Better Than You Found It

My brother Dwarka enjoyed a good career. After graduating from the Thapar Institute of Engineering and Technology in Patiala, Dwarka joined the Punjab government as a Civil Engineer for irrigation projects. Initially, he worked as an engineer on the Bhakhra Dam, one of the high-priority Five-Year Plan projects of the Indian government. The objective of this dam was to minimize the devastating effects of the waters of two rivers during monsoons while harnessing the power of water as electricity and putting the water to good use irrigating crops. It took a long time, but the work has paid off. There are fewer floods, and the crop output in this region has increased significantly.

Subsequently, Dwarka worked on developing irrigation systems and building canals in Punjab. He was selected to go to Iraq from 1976 to 1981 to help that country build efficient irrigation systems. Bauji was so proud of his son for helping make a difference in the lives of people on a global scale. But he was perhaps proudest of the fact that Dwarka turned out to be an enormously generous person.

Dwarka was highly inspired by words Bauji repeated often: "You will not be remembered by what you had but by what you gave to those in need." These words affected all of us, but none as much as Dwarka, who'd been born with an especially kind heart.

One small example is when we were going to school together in Varpal. One day we were walking home when a hailstorm ambushed us. The hail was golf ball sized and there was no place to hide. We laid down on the ground and covered our heads with our hands, but that was not helping much, and we were getting pelted. Dwarka then laid on top of me so that he would bear the brunt of the hailstorm. I was safe from the rest of the barrage, but not Dwarka. When it was all over, I could see that welts and lacerations covered his back. I am sure he was in tremendous pain, but he did not complain as we continued walking after the storm passed.

Dwarka married Kamlesh who was a schoolteacher. They made a good team. Both of them helped the poor as much as they could. I recall witnessing a particularly extreme example of their generosity during one visit to see them after I had moved to the States. Dwarka had built a nice house with the savings he had from working in Iraq. Next to his home was an empty lot. As we walked by the lot one day, Dwarka noticed that a poor family of four had set up a little tent. The father was ironing clothes, the mother was trying to cook something for the children, and the two children were playing in the dirt.

The family had no running water, no place to go to the bathroom, and no place to sleep. It was cold outside and the children had no warm clothes.

Dwarka walked up to the father and offered the family a place to stay in his new home.

"We have a garage that you can turn into an apartment. Your children will be safe and warm. We have a room above the garage, if you prefer that. The roof is flat; your children will be able to play on the roof. Over a period of time, we can build additional space for your family as the children get older."

The father was taken aback. "Sir, I do not have money to pay rent," he said politely.

Dwarka responded quickly. "I am not expecting you to pay me any rent."

Dwarka and his children helped the poor family move into the garage. For many years after that day, Dwarka and his family contributed to educating the children and ensured that they had food and clothing.

Unfortunately, Dwarka passed away at the age of sixty-five from a freak accident. Word of his death passed quickly among all of those he had helped over the years. More than a thousand people showed up at Dwarka's funeral, and for many days afterward, people continued to come from all over India to pay their respects.

As that remarkable turnout attests, every part of the world Dwarka touched was improved by his interaction with it. He changed lives directly and indirectly, so many lives that people felt compelled to travel long distances to celebrate him after he was gone. He lived his entire life by one of Bauji's axioms: that it was essential to leave a place better than you found it. What Bauji meant by this was that it wasn't enough for you to thrive or even for you and your family to thrive. A person's mission should always be to contribute to the community at large, to make the world around them a better place.

Dwarka had to work for his education and to establish his career. Once he reaped the benefits of that hard work, he could have concentrated his money and his time on an insulated circle of people. But he knew that this wasn't the right way to live, so he extended his reach as far as his resources would take him.

This is a guideline we all can live by. Whether it is your neighborhood, your office, your school system, or any other part of the common space you share with others, taking responsibility to make even the littlest improvement to any of these places enhances the lives of all involved, including yourself. And good deeds of this sort are often contagious. For example, if you decided to try to make your child's school better by volunteering a few hours of your time a week, there is a good chance you'll inspire others to do the same. How much better will that make your child's school? How much better will that be for your child? And, if we were all operating on this principle, just imagine how much we could accomplish.

# Exercise 13: Personal Impact Exercise

Imagine that you are retired from work, sitting in a rocking chair, and looking back at your life. A faint smile appears on your face as you look at your life in the rearview mirror. You are happy and satisfied as you reflect on years past because you believe:

- "I had a clear sense of purpose in my life to positively influence the life of people around me."
- "I had a clear plan to make a positive impact on others."
- "I was committed to bettering myself throughout my life. I learned from the past and focused on the future."
- "I shared my knowledge freely."
- "I helped many people and made a positive difference in the lives of those I met during my life and career."
- "People remember me fondly as a friend, helper, and a mentor."

If you agree with each of the above statements, great! If not, you have time to plan and act now in order to have that feeling when you retire and reflect on your life.

# Principle #14: Encourage Your Children to Fly as High as They Can

When my youngest sister Usha was a child, it was a transitional period for women and education in India. Only a small percentage of young girls went to school and a very small percentage of those girls went to college. Back then, girls were essentially raised to become good wives and mothers, and attempting to go beyond these parameters was risky. Most Indian men were very intimidated by highly educated women and often chose to seek marriage partners elsewhere.

In spite of these conditions, Bauji encouraged Usha to get as much education as possible. Usha was a bright girl and did extremely well in school from her first day. In fact, she was such a good student that she jumped a couple of grades in elementary school to finish fourth grade at the age of eight. Bauji, being the headmaster of the elementary school in Pandori during the time Usha was one of the students, saw tremendous potential in her and encouraged her to go into the medical field and become a doctor. During this period of India's development, not many women went into the medical field or were selected to join the few available seats in medical colleges. When Usha completed high school, it was time to decide whether she should choose to be a doctor, an engineer, or a teacher. Bauji encouraged her to take the entrance exam for medical school. He accompanied Usha to the central location where hundreds of aspiring doctors were taking the entrance exam only to find that she was the only female taking the exam. The prospect of being the only woman was at best dispiriting for both Usha and Bauji. Disheartened, Usha abandoned the thought of becoming a doctor and instead got her Master of Science degree in chemistry and became a teacher.

Once Usha was out of college, it was time for her to be married. According to Indian customs, this meant it was her family's job to find a suitable husband for her. That would turn out to be a challenge for Usha and for the entire family.

By tradition, the parents of a young woman of marriageable age, or their proxy, would approach the parents of a particular young man to see if there was interest in a match. If the parents were interested, the parents and the man would come over to the meet the woman. The woman would be required to prepare a meal and be sociable. The purpose of this meeting was twofold: to see if there was indeed a cultural match and to confirm that the woman had the requisite household talents (as I've already mentioned, the social mores were very different then). The only "talent" the man needed to exhibit was the ability to provide financial support for his new family after the marriage.

Since Usha was already well-educated and was self-sufficient financially, she was not a typical young woman willing to abide by obsolete customs. She rightfully thought that these customs were demeaning. "It is like somebody is trying to buy a horse, not select a future spouse," I remember her saying. "And the shame of it all is that the girl's family is the one who pays for it all." She was referring to the dowry system that required the woman's family to make a sizeable gift to get the couple started on their life together: buying them a house or a car, clothes, and enough money for them to live comfortably for a year or two until the couple could support themselves.

Usha rebelled against the system and refused to be "interviewed" by potential marriage partners and their families. Though it complicated matters considerably, Bauji, who had a long history of challenging conventions, supported her.

"You can be both highly educated and self-sufficient and also be a good wife and mother," he told her. "There is no better feeling than being a parent and helping your children grow and develop into excellent human beings. Imagine what you can do. You are an exceptionally bright woman. You can be a great wife and mother."

Bauji knew that, at the time, being a great wife and mother was likely to curtail Usha's career aspirations, and he felt it was important to help her deal with this and to accept tradition rather than face the hardship of challenging those traditions with intransigence.

"I am sorry," he said. "I can't change the Indian culture and customs overnight. The day will come when girls are not subjected to such humiliation and the dowry system will become a thing of the past. Until then, we must accept and live within the culture as is. I urge you to find acceptance in your heart and at least meet with potential suitors."

With constant encouragement and the loving support of her entire family, Usha finally relented and married Harish Dhall, a banker.

The encouragement my father always provided—as well as her tremendous innate talents—allowed Usha the ability to accomplish all of her goals. She was successful professionally, continuing to teach after her marriage and finally becoming a high school principal. And, even though she never completely bowed to convention, she became a dedicated wife and an exceptional mother. After she got married, she lived in a joint family environment with her in-laws. She would get up at 4:00 a.m., get breakfast ready for the entire family, and travel by three modes of transportation, which included riding a bike to the bus stand, taking a bus to the town where she taught, and then walking to the school where she taught. After she got home late in the evening, she cooked dinner for the family and then spent time with her three children to help them study. And, following the model she learned from our father, she encouraged each of her children to fly high with great results.

Her eldest son, Rohit, is a brilliant neurologist. He received his medical degree from a highly recognized institute in India, then came to the United States and, motivated by his father's Parkinson's disease, completed his education in neurology and has further specialized in the field of moving disorders.

Usha's second son, Rahul, finished his undergrad in chemical engineering and came to the US for postgraduate studies at Louisiana Tech University. After a couple of quarters at LTU, he transferred to The Ohio State University, where he finished his MS in food science and nutrition. After working for a few months in the US, he decided to return to India.

Usha's daughter, KnuPriya, finished her college degree, married a nice, hard-working young man and is living in Luxembourg.

During her life, Usha truly lived Bauji's messages. She helped everybody in her extended family, and she coached and guided her children to achieve their potential.

Throughout her life, Usha was a model of and a messenger for one of Bauji's most important lessons: encourage your children to fly as high as they can. Despite the limitations she faced when she was growing up, she accomplished so much more than most of her contemporaries because she always felt supported. Just imagine what she would have missed if she had not capitalized on my father's encouragement to make the most of her education or if she had been so committed to flouting tradition that she never had the family that gave her so much joy. Bauji knew that Usha was special in so many ways, and he made sure that she knew it as well so she could be everything that she was meant to be.

This is a lesson that has value for all of us. Yes, I realize that not every reader of this book has children or will have children in the future. But nearly every reader will have some young person in their lives who can benefit from the presence of someone who believes in them. There are two parts of this, and both are essential. The first part is the simple act of offering encouragement. If a young person shares a dream with you, be sure to validate that dream. Sure, the dream itself might be unrealistic for the person involved (I recently met a girl who claimed she wanted to be a surgeon, even though she also admitted that she was nauseated by the sight of blood), but your first job is to help this person feel good about dreaming. Then we come to the second part, which is where you provide resources and assistance to help that person fly as high as possible. In the case of our blood-averse wannabe surgeon, maybe this comes in the form of an introduction to others in the medical profession who might help her find a part of the field that does not involve cutting or surgery. Or maybe it's by having a series of conversations with this person where you discover what is most appealing to her about being a surgeon and then introducing her to fields in other disciplines that might give her the same sense of accomplishment without making her sick to her stomach.

I know my sister Usha never forgot the tremendous boost my father gave her. The young people in your life will regard you the same way.

## Exercise 14: Help and encourage somebody to fly higher!

I am sure you know somebody in your circle who could benefit from your advice, encouragement, or help. It could be your own child, a friend's child, or a student who is feeling down or needs financial help to complete his/her education.

- Identify at least one such candidate who can benefit from your life experiences and encouragement.
- Proactively approach the person and listen to figure out what he or she really needs.
- Guide and help the individual to set higher goals.
- Provide your time and/or other resources such as financial assistance to help achieve the set goals.
- Follow up and spend time with the individual to provide continued encouragement and to build confidence.

# Principle #15: Do Your Best; the Universe Will Do the Rest

When I finished high school, before I made the decision to attend DAV College, I had no idea what I wanted to do with the rest of my life, but I saw an ad in the state newspaper about joining the Indian Air Force. This seemed appealing to me, especially since I was only fifteen and hadn't committed yet to continuing my education.

I told Bauji that I was going to try to enlist in the Air Force. "It is a great opportunity," I said. "I get a free four-year education at the end of which I will become a second lieutenant."

Bauji did not know anything more about military service in India than I did, so he concurred. I took a written exam at one of the test centers in Amritsar and did extremely well. Because of this, the Air Force invited me to come for an extended personal interview in Dehradun, which was about a day's train ride from our village in Pandori.

When I got to Dehradun, I found that there were more than forty students competing for four available spots. I'd been facing similar odds my entire life, so I wasn't intimidated by these odds. In fact, the competitiveness in me kicked in. Whether I wanted to be in the Air Force or not (and at this point, I was not entirely sure), I was going to compete to the best of my ability.

As it turned out, I was the youngest and the shortest candidate. Having spent most of my time around family and living in small places, I knew very little about the bigger world and I had few life experiences to draw upon. I would hear the other candidates talk about their experiences, and I could barely relate. Most of them were sons of military members, and several had fathers in the Air Force. They had travelled. They knew things I had no idea of. I felt embarrassed, inadequate, and alone. However, I wanted to win.

The interview consisted of another written exam, physical tests, and psychological tests. I made it through the written test with flying colors, coming out with the top scores among all the candidates.

Next came the physical tests. We were taken to an obstacle course, where we had to go through various exercises within a set time. After that, we were tested on specific military problems such as crossing a river with only a rope and a few bamboo poles. I did relatively well on the individual physical tests, but the military-specific tests were an extreme challenge for me.

The psychological tests came on the last day. At first, they showed us slides with various images and asked us to write about our interpretation of these images. A psychologist then spent two hours with each of us, probing us with many questions.

When it was time for my session with the psychologist, I felt a bit ambushed. He bombarded me with questions, asking me to give the first answers that came to my mind. After this barrage, he asked, "If you do not get selected for the Air Force, what will you do?" While I realized at this point that I was facing some stiff competition, I was adamant. "I am certain I will be selected for the Air Force," I replied several times.

The psychologist was patient with me, but he finally insisted that I give him a second choice. "If I cannot be in the Air Force, I would like to be a scientist," I said at last.

The psychologist put his arm around my shoulders and said, "Son, go pursue that field. You are made to be a scientist." And in that moment, I realized that he was right. Attempting to get into the Air Force was about my reluctance to commit to a field of study that would make the most of my innate talents. Science was my real calling.

I returned to Amritsar to attend DAV College. After college, I needed to get a technical education. I applied for admission to a completely new institute in Karnal called the National Dairy Research Institute (NDRI). There was a lot of buzz in the country that India was planning to become self-sufficient in food and nutrition and, since more than ninety percent of the Indian population was vegetarian, the protein for their nutrition would come primarily from milk. This institute was created to increase the production and preservation of milk and milk products through technology. I found this pursuit extremely appealing.

Entry to NDRI required a written examination and a personal interview with the selection committee. Six thousand applicants took the written exam, after which three hundred moved forward to the personal interview. I aced the written examination and was invited to the interview, where I learned that I was the highest-ranking candidate. I asked about tuition and the cost of room and board and was stunned with the answer. The tuition was the equivalent of Bauji's entire salary; there would be nothing left to feed the family. This was deflating, as I realized that I could not possibly accept admission to NDRI if offered. I gave everything I could to excelling at the interview, but when I returned to Amritsar, I announced to my family that I would not accept an admission offer.

As the last day for admission offers passed, the point seemed to be moot. No offer from NDRI seemed to be forthcoming. With no alternative left, I decided to go back to DAV College to major in chemistry. I went to Bauji for the tuition money. I could tell that he was not happy, but he gave me a hundred-rupee note to pay my fees. I went to the college, paid the sixty-rupee entrance charge, and came back with the remaining forty rupees.

I will never forget what happened after that. My entire family had shown up to stay at my brother's tiny apartment in Amritsar due to a potential armed conflict between India and Pakistan. Bauji was there impatiently pacing. Cramped into this little place, I could hardly move. I decided I would start studying so that I would be able to get good marks in college, even though this college was not my ideal school. I was doing my homework using an inkpot and an old-style ink pen. I had tried returning the forty rupees to Bauji, but he waved me off. I set down the paper currency on the table next to my inkpot and, as luck would have it, the inkpot turned over and spilled the ink on the money.

This was a tipping point for my father. He unleashed all of the anger that had been building up inside of him. How could his son let him down and not gain admission to NDRI? I could feel his stare, his disappointment, as he launched into me, mimicking my voice and repeating what I had told the family, "I *will not accept the offer of admission from this institute,*" he said, imitating me. "Next time, wait for the invitation before you decline!"

I wanted to disappear, but there was nowhere to go. The earth refused to open up to provide me an escape route. Instead, I buried my head in my hands.

And then a postman came to the door and announced that there was a telegram for me. I found this baffling. Who would send me a telegram? I opened the envelope with trembling hands and let out a shriek—it was an offer of admission from NDRI!

Later, I learned the reasons for my delayed acceptance at the Institute. During that period of time, corruption in India was the norm. Since the seats in this batch were limited to only thirty, most of them were taken by the sons and other relatives of well-connected politicians. After these boys got into the school, they soon realized that the classes and the related work, such as taking care of dairy animals, was very hard. Several of them returned to their homes within a couple of weeks, thereby vacating seats for merit-based candidates. I happened to be one of three merit-based candidates selected, and the three of us joined the classes almost three weeks after the school had already started.

The first hurdle of being selected as a candidate for the institute was over. The financial hurdle of high cost still loomed ahead. I soon learned that a company-sponsored merit scholarship was to be awarded to the student who scored the highest grades during the first year of classes. This was the only solution to my financial issue. As previously described, I resolved that I would study hard to earn that scholarship—and I did. I earned that scholarship every year for the four years, sparing my family from the financial hardship of supporting my technical education.

This experience was more stressful than I would have liked it to be, but it proved a very important lesson: that if you do everything you possibly can to succeed at something, good fortune is likely to take you the rest of the way. I had invested every bit of my effort into gaining acceptance to NDRI. Even after I realized the financial demands were going to be too great for my family, I continued to present myself as an ideal candidate to the selection committee. In the end, even though the tuition was well beyond our means, the effort I had made had allowed for a situation to arise where I could still go to the school and protect my parents from the potential financial hardship.

The important takeaway here is that effort leads to opportunity. Have there been times in your life when you have avoided pursuing something because the odds were against you or because others convinced you that the pursuit was too difficult? How many of those things did you *really* want? How different would your life be now if you had found a way to achieve them?

I am not talking about dumb luck. I did not get into NDRI because I won a lottery. I got in because, even though my financial situation was dire, I exemplified what they were looking for in a candidate. The same could very well be true for any pursuit you are currently considering. Are the odds against you? They very well might be, but your desire and your talents might prove you to be above the odds. Is the road to success too challenging? That could be the case, but if your will is strong and if you want this thing badly enough, you might discover help you never anticipated to overcome these challenges.

One of the things that Bauji always emphasized, and something I have experienced repeatedly throughout my life, is that the universe rewards effort. That is a critical thing for you to keep in mind when you decide which dreams to pursue.

## Exercise 15: Know yourself!

Knowing one's own strengths and weaknesses is one of the most important prerequisites of a successful life.

A psychological model called the Johari Window helps us understand and improve ourselves in the following manner:

- THE OPEN SELF: Our strengths and weaknesses that are known to us and known to others.
- THE HIDDEN SELF: Our strengths and weaknesses known to us but not known to others.
- THE BLIND SELF: Our strengths and weaknesses known to others but not known to us.
- THE UNKNOWN SELF: Neither known to us nor known to others.

In order to know and understand our different selves, we need to spend time with ourselves as well as with others to get a complete picture.

Here is an exercise to cultivate and leverage a better understanding of self-awareness:

- Spend time with yourself daily without any distraction.
- Record your observations and insights.
- Become a better observer and listener by practicing.
- Ask others for feedback such as:
    o Which of my actions and behaviors inspire you?
    o Which of my actions and behaviors need modifications?

# Principle #16:
# Hard Work Is the Only Path to Your Desired Destination

For as long as I could remember, Bauji had instilled in us a commitment to hard work. He knew that the outside world was not going to do us any favors and that we were going to have to prove ourselves repeatedly if we wanted to accomplish our goals. And, regardless of our intelligence or our innate talents, the only way someone from the poor little village of Pandori was ever going to be able to prove him or herself was by exhibiting an unparalleled work ethic.

This message became even clearer to me when I moved to the United States to pursue my postgraduate degree at The Ohio State University. I joined the university as a graduate student in the Department of Dairy Technology, and my adviser was a young assistant professor, Dr. Poul M.T. Hansen. Dr. Hansen was originally from Denmark. He was a recent graduate of the University of Illinois and wanted to make his mark so that he could be promoted to associate professor and earn tenure. His grad students bore the brunt of his ambition. We all worked twelve hours a day, six days a week for a stipend of $225 per month. We were also students, which meant going to classes and doing homework that added another six hours a day. Some felt overwhelmed by this schedule but, having Bauji's work ethic ingrained in me, I was fine getting by with three or four hours of sleep a night.

Most of the friends I had at the beginning of my time at Ohio State were from India with nothing else to do but study, work, eat, and sleep. At the graduate school level, if we fell below a B average for two successive quarters, we would be expelled from the university and would have to find our way back to India. I trembled at the thought of having to go back home without getting my PhD. *My family has spent all their financial resources to send me here,* I would think. *How would I face them if I don't succeed?* I made sure that was never an issue, always working hard enough to get excellent grades.

I also wanted to impress Poul Hansen since he had entrusted me with his work. I would get up at 5 a.m., get ready, make a cheese sandwich for my lunch, and take the two-mile walk to the Department of Food Science and Nutrition. I would start working on my research experiment as soon as I arrived. Dr. Hansen often showed up around the same time, and he very quickly became a strong supporter of mine.

Once I completed my MS, it was time for me to decide what my next step would be. Should I go back to India to look for a job, or should I continue my studies and finish my PhD? My parents expected me to come home. I was twenty-four years old and, in their minds, I had enough education to get a good job in India. They believed I should get married and settle down back in my home country.

But going home at that point didn't match my larger goals and it didn't align with the lessons Bau-ji had been teaching me since I was a child. I had gone to the US to complete my PhD. That was what I needed to do. I would go home to India after that and get an R&D position in the industry or work at a university as a professor.

I enrolled in the PhD program and was assigned to Dr. Emil Mikolajcik as his research assistant. Dr. Mikolajcik, fondly known as "Dr. Mike," was work-ing on understanding the protective properties of human milk. I found the subject to be fascinating. The possibility of clarifying how mother's milk pro-vided protection to a baby against early-stage infec-tions felt like a noble endeavor. The work was engag-ing, and as a bonus, Dr. Mike agreed to increase my pay from $225 per month to $250.

Once I had received my PhD, I worked as a post-doc with Dr. Hansen for about a year and then was fortunate enough to land a research job at the Quak-er Oats Company. To my surprise, my job title was Group Leader. However, when I joined the compa-ny, I quickly learned that the group I was "leading" consisted of just me.

Once again, it was time to push my work ethic to the limits. Driven to be one of the best research sci-entists at the company, I would get up early in the morning, get to the lab, and conduct multiple sets of experiments to see which would be deserving of further study. I would continue to work by myself into the late hours of the night, finishing up between 1 a.m. and 2 a.m. I then would go home and return to the lab around 7 a.m. I had been working hard for as long as I could remember, but never this hard. Fortunately, the effort paid off, and I was able to develop a number of new products including soymilk, soy cheese, and soy-based meats termed "sausage analog," "bacon analog," and even "steak analog." Within two years after joining Quaker, I had more than fifteen patents and more than fifteen publications to my name.

All the success I had later in my career can be sourced back to the strong start that my work ethic gave me. Once I got to the US, I had a clear set of goals and an absolute commitment to push myself as strenuously as I needed in order to reach those goals.

I cannot endorse this approach to pursuing your dreams enough. In my experience, there are very few "lucky breaks" out there. Yes, sometimes good fortune just falls in your lap. Overwhelmingly, though, luck is a byproduct of clear ambitions and an absolute dedication to the work. And this is as true about any pursuit that matters to you—your role as a parent, your role as a student, your role as a friend—as it is true of career ambitions.

If you want it, you are going to have to work for it. But if you work for it, there is a good chance that the work will pay off.

## Exercise 16: Hard work and success

- What are your key insights and takeaways from the story in this chapter?
- Based on your personal experiences and observations of others, what is your belief about the relationship between hard work and success?
- What inspires you about this chapter?
- What will you do differently tomorrow to increase your chances of success in life?

# Afterword

I can think of no greater testament to Bauji's wisdom than to say that his lessons have guided me throughout my entire life and continue to do so today. I certainly haven't lived a perfect life (is that even possible?) but I think by any reasonable measure I have led a good and successful one, and that is a direct result of the teachings I have passed along here.

On the professional side, the lesson from my father that has served me the most over time has been, "Set high goals and work hard to achieve them." After I had been in the business world for a while, I realized that if I wanted to have greater success in developing products and bringing them to market, I was going to need to understand the marketplace better than I did at that time. So, even though I already had a PhD in a scientific discipline that aligned with my profession, I enrolled at the University of Chicago to get my MBA in finance and marketing.

This had a near-immediate effect on my career arc. With this additional education, I was able to analyze the business impact of my scientific work and present it to the other business functions and my boss in a cogent fashion. This led me to abandon some of the projects I had been developing that were not in line with the business strategy or capabilities of the company. The impact of my work on the business was getting recognized, and I started feeling more and more confident that I could make a difference in the growth of our company.

The feeling of excitement drove me to put in long hours at the office. I would work on my projects in the laboratory during the day to test the scientific hypothesis. In the evening and late at night, I would work in the pilot plant to see if the prototypes I had developed in the lab could be commercialized. The joy of seeing the results was almost intoxicating.

This combination of skills took me on a path that included a management role at Quaker Oats, Senior Vice President of Research and Development at PepsiCo, President of Consumer Products R&D at Warner Lambert, and, ultimately Chief Innovation Officer at the Wm. Wrigley Jr. Company. I retired from Wrigley at the age of sixty-three, having helped the company build its business from two billion dollars in revenues to five billion dollars.

After a short break from the corporate world, I started a consulting firm, Arora Innovations, LLC. The company specializes in working with clients to help accelerate business growth and build exceptional leadership teams to sustain momentum in their organizations for generations to come. It has been quite gratifying to see the development of excellent leaders who, in turn, have driven growth of their businesses and their people.

On the personal side, as I write this, my wife Janet and I have been married for forty-six years. In 1977, I became a US citizen. A year later, Janet and I were blessed with a son, Daven. Daven has extended this blessing through his wife Julie and their three children, Angel, Krishan, and Kareena. We are financially secure, and we have been able to help a number of family members on both sides of our family. In addition, we have built and funded a foundation designed to help deserving students complete their education and to support people who have fallen on hard times and need financial aid.

When Daven and I visited Pandori and I saw the regard in which the villagers held my father even thirty years after his death, I fully realized how universal Bauji's messages truly were. His legacy extended beyond his family to the transformation of an entire village. He had a powerful effect on the lives of so many people, even those who had only known him for a brief period. And I am absolutely convinced that his teachings will have an effect on you as well. As my friend Cheri Warren said to me when I told her I was considering writing this book, "The wisdom, the ideals, and the principles of your father belong to the world."

I hope you have found inspiration in the lessons of my father. If you have, please pass his messages along to others. You know now what they have done for my family and what they have done for my village. I can only imagine what they can do for you and anyone who chooses to learn and pursue the principles and insights of Bauji, a village teacher who left a lasting legacy of helping his family, his village, and the many other people who knew him.

# Acknowledgments

I am grateful to my parents, Kanshi Ram and Kailash Wanti, for being the model parents. Their hard work and personal sacrifice paved the way for my siblings and me to have happy and successful lives.

Compiling the contents of this book would not have been possible without the help of many of my family members. Their vivid recollection of the events of the Partition of India provided the basis for most of the writing about the early years. My brother Om sat tirelessly with me to share his memories and to inspire me to continue writing. My brothers and sisters have always been there for me during my trying times. I am thankful to Om, Pushpa, Dwarka, and Usha for their help and their unconditional love throughout my life.

Along the way, many people have put their hands on my shoulders and helped me on my path. Some of those people do not even know or realize how valuable their guidance has been for me. Notable among them are Dr. Ashok Ganguly for urging me to pursue my education in the United States; Wayne Calloway, Roger Enrico, David Novak, Dennis Heard, and Bennett Nussbaum who were my mentors at PepsiCo; and Beau Wrigley who I admire as one of the best young leaders of his time. My dear wife, Janet, has been by my side on this life journey for the last forty-six years. Janet and I are blessed to have a terrific son, Daven, who has helped with the content and layout of this book and has provided steadfast support and inspiration to me personally and professionally. I have derived inspiration from the life of my terrific friend Mohinder Chanana, whose values and family focus have been the guiding lights for me. The exceptional progress of several generations of my parents' descendants all over the world speaks volumes for the value of my father's principles and insights, and has been the key reason for me to write this book.

My daughter-in-law Julie, my son Daven, and my friend Lou Aronica deserve extra special thanks for their help with editing and polishing the contents of this book to make it worthy of publication. I am also indebted to Candace Shaffer for her valuable copy editing and guidance. The enthusiasm and support of my family and friends throughout this project have been extremely helpful in keeping me energized. The unconditional love of our three grandchildren—Angel, Krishan, and Kareena—has motivated me throughout this journey. I certainly hope that the principles of my father articulated in this book will help them lead a happy and fulfilling life.